THE RAPHAEL
TAPESTRY CARTOONS

THE
Raphael
Tapestry Cartoons

NARRATIVE · DECORATION · DESIGN

Sharon Fermor

SCALA BOOKS
IN ASSOCIATION WITH
THE VICTORIA AND ALBERT MUSEUM

Text and illustrations
© The Board of Trustees of the Victoria and Albert Museum 1996

First published in 1996 by Scala Books
an imprint of Philip Wilson Publishers Limited
143–149 Great Portland Street
London WIN 5FB

Distributed in the USA and Canada by Antique Collectors' Club
Market Street Industrial Park, Wappinger's Falls
New York 12590

All rights reserved
ISBN 1 85759 055 4

Designed and typeset by Malcolm Preskett
Edited by Diana de Froment
Printed and bound in Italy by Sfera International, Milan

PHOTOGRAPHIC CREDITS

Victoria and Albert Museum, London.
The Royal Collection. Copyright 1996 Her Majesty Queen Elizabeth II:
figs 1, 2, 3, 4, 5, 6, 7

Vatican Museums, Rome:
figs 8, 28, 29, 30, 31, 32, 38, 39, 40, 41, 42, 43, 44, 45, 46, 47, 48, 49, 50, 51

Victoria and Albert Museum, London. Courtesy of the Board of Trustees:
figs 9, 16, 17, 18, 19, 20

Los Angeles County Museum of Art. Copyright 1996 Museum Associates,
Los Angeles County Museum of Art: fig. 10

British Museum, London. Courtesy of the Trustees: fig. 12

Scala, Florence: figs 14, 23, 33, 34

Royal Library, Windsor Castle. The Royal Collection.
Copyright 1996 Her Majesty Queen Elizabeth II: figs 36, 37

CONTENTS

PREFACE

THE Raphael tapestry cartoons are among the most important surviving examples of Renaissance art. As designs for tapestry, they are unique in Raphael's *oeuvre*. They are also the earliest surviving tapestry cartoons on paper. These facts, together with their long and complex history, make them of enormous interest and significance within the history of art. They are also works of singular beauty and dramatic power.

The Victoria and Albert Museum is privileged to have the cartoons on loan from Her Majesty Queen Elizabeth II. In 1992 they were taken off display to allow for essential refurbishment of the gallery. This gave conservators and curators an invaluable opportunity to learn more about the cartoons which had not been removed from the wall for about thirty years. In that time, not only has art-historical scholarship advanced, especially in the study of cartoons, but investigative technologies have become increasingly refined allowing us to make in-depth analyses of the cartoons that would not have been possible in the 1960s. The present book is in part a result of this recent campaign of conservation and restoration, and aims to give an overview of its most significant findings. It also aims to use those findings to extend our understanding of the cartoons' history and to place them in a wider context.

Any study of the cartoons is indebted to John Shearman's magisterial monograph of 1972 and the present book is no exception. Its aim is in no way to replace Professor Shearman's text, which remains fundamental, but to review the cartoons in the light of new research and in a briefer format.

Many people have contributed to the project from which this book arises and my thanks go to them all. I would particularly like to thank staff of the Royal Collection Trust, especially Alan Donnithorne, Christopher Lloyd and Jane Roberts, for their co-operation and support. Thanks are also due to Carmen Bambach, Simon Barnes, John Bowman, Mary Butler, Peter Cannon-Brookes, Josephine Darrah, Wendy Hefford, Susan Lambert, Momart plc., Arnold Nesselrath, James Edwin Newman and Agfa-Gevaert Ltd, Howard Pearson, Plowman, Craven and Associates, Michael Podro, Peter Riley, John Shearman, John Steer, Timothy Stevens, Stone Foundries Ltd, John Wagstaff and Ian Whinstanley. Photographs of the cartoons were provided by Sara Hodges, Mike Kitcatt and Paul Robins of the Victoria and Albert Photographic Studio.

I owe a particular debt of gratitude to Alan Derbyshire with whom I have worked closely and happily throughout the project. Some of the ideas and discoveries incorporated here are his and I have derived great benefit from our countless discussions on the cartoons.

Sharon Fermor
London 1996

1

History and Status

1. J. Shearman, *Raphael's Cartoons in the collection of Her Majesty the Queen and the Tapestries for the Sistine Chapel*, London, 1972, p.3. Shearman has discussed the cartoons and tapestries more recently in his *Only Connect...Art and the Spectator in the Italian Renaissance*, Princeton, 1992, pp.202–7, 216–8, 223, 238–9, 252–3.

2. For the decoration of the Chapel under Sixtus see L. Ettlinger, *The Sistine Chapel before Michelangelo*, Oxford, 1965. For the history and decoration of the Chapel more generally see C. Pietrangeli et al., *The Sistine Chapel. The Art, the History and the Restoration*, New York, 1986.

THE cartoons were commissioned from Raphael (Raffaello Sanzio) in 1515 by the Medici Pope, Leo X (1513–21), as designs for tapestries to hang in the Sistine Chapel in the Vatican, Rome. The commission was one of exceptional importance for Leo, not least because it was his one opportunity to make a significant visible mark on the decoration of the Papal Chapel, which has been described as 'the first chapel in Christendom'.[1] Recently built by Pope Sixtus IV (1471–84) on the site of an earlier chapel, it was reserved primarily for the use of the Pope and his immediate entourage. It stood in the heart of the Vatican, a complex of buildings which formed the residence of the Popes. The Vatican's importance reflected in part the immense power of the Pope as head of the universal Roman Catholic church and also a secular prince and statesman, involved in international politics.

Sixtus himself had had the upper walls frescoed in 1481–82, by a team of the most prestigious contemporary artists, including Botticelli, Signorelli, Ghirlandaio, Cosimo Rosselli and Perugino.[2] The vault had been painted by Michelangelo, eight years Raphael's senior, for Leo's predecessor, Pope Julius II, in 1508–12. The main area remaining on which Leo could make his mark was that of the lower walls, already painted for Sixtus IV with fictive tapestries in gold and silver emblazoned with his della Rovere family emblems. It is perhaps not surprising that Leo decided to cover these with the luxury ~~~ of a major set of real tapestries, appropriate to the status of the place. At the same time, Leo was following an established tradition of decorating Papal churches with tapestries.[3]

The subject-matter of the tapestries was fully in line with the earlier decoration of the Chapel, and especially the side-walls which display typological fresco cycles of *The Lives of Christ and Moses*.[4] The frescoes present Moses as a divinely appointed precursor to, or antetype of, Christ and compare their respective deeds in a complex way. They thus assert the continuity of power from the Old Testament to the New, and the cycle ends with Perugino's fresco of *Christ giving the Keys to Peter*, making clear the legitimacy and history of the authority of the Pope, as the descendant of St Peter. Above were painted figures of the early Popes, also for Sixtus IV, extending the theme of Papal continuity.

The subjects of the tapestries are taken from the New Testament, particularly episodes from the lives of St Peter and St Paul. They focus on those which make a specific point, primarily 'the pre-eminence of the Roman Church...derived from its foundation jointly by the two Princes of the Apostles, and consecrated by their joint Roman martyrdom'.[5]

The scenes represented for which cartoons survive are: *The Miraculous Draught of Fishes* (Luke 5: 3–10) (fig.7); *Christ's Charge to Peter* (John 21: 15–17) (fig.8); *The Healing of the Lame Man* (Acts 3: 1–11) (fig.9); *The Death of Ananias* (Acts 5: 1–6) (fig.10); *The Conversion of the Proconsul* (Acts 13: 6–12) (fig.11); *The Sacrifice at Lystra* (Acts 14: 8–18) (fig.12) and *Paul Preaching at Athens* (Acts 17: 15–34) (fig.13). Other subjects extant as tapestries for which the cartoons are lost are: *The Conversion of Saul* (Acts 9: 1–7), (fig.1) *The Stoning of Stephen* (Acts 9: 1–7) and *Paul in Prison* (Acts 16: 23–6.). Thus, five of the scenes focus on the life of St Paul, four on that of St Peter and one on St Stephen. Through these scenes, Peter and Paul are portrayed as the twin founders of the Christian Church, with special missions to convert the Jews and the Gentiles respectively. They are also presented as the joint sources of the Pope's own authority and the tapestries were certainly intended to have a personal and political dimension for Leo in his role as Pope.

The number of tapestries which Leo intended for the Chapel is uncertain. Curiously the ten which survive, generally assumed to be the intended number, are too few to furnish the entire lower space of the Chapel and yet one too many to cover the area inside the *cancellata*, or chancel-screen. In the most plausible order suggested so far one tapestry, *Paul Preaching at Athens*, would have hung alone in the area outside the *cancellata*, which divided the chapel into two.[6] However, such an

3. Shearman, *Raphael's Cartoons*, pp.4–5.

4. For the interpretation of these frescoes see particularly Ettlinger, op. cit., passim.

5. Shearman, op. cit., p.61.

6. This is the view taken by Shearman in *Raphael's Cartoons*, Ch.2.

7. The question of the hanging order has also been discussed by Creighton Gilbert, who refutes Shearman's argument in 'Are the ten tapestries a complete series or a fragment?', *Studi su Raffaello; atti del congresso internazionale di studi*, Urbino-Florence, 1984, pp.533–50.

Fig. 1. After Raphael
The Conversion of Saul
Tapestry, 4.6 x 5.4m
Vatican Museums, Rome

arrangement would have been both asymmetrical and idiosyncratic, and it seems somewhat surprising that such an important and prestigious decorative scheme should have been left apparently incomplete.[7] Other subjects which one might have expected to find in the cycle, such as the martyrdoms of Peter and Paul, could also have been included in a larger tapestry set.

There is some evidence to suggest that Leo may have originally intended to have sixteen tapestries. In July 1517 Cardinal Luigi d'Aragona, while journeying through Europe, visited the workshop of Pieter van Aelst in Brussels where the Leonine tapestries were being made. His secretary, Antonio de Beatis, kept a diary of the journey and recorded that the party was shown the tapestries which the Pope was having woven for the Chapel. De Beatis wrote: 'Here [in Brussels] Pope

Leo is having made XVI pieces of tapestry, it is said for the Chapel of Sixtus which is in the Apostolic Palace in Rome, for the most part of silk and gold; the price is two thousand gold ducats a piece. We were on the spot to see them in progress, and one piece of the story of *The Donation of the Keys,* which is very fine, we saw complete…'.[8] While completely to clothe the walls of the Sistine Chapel may have required seventeen tapestries, sixteen corresponds to the number of frescoes on the upper walls.[9] If the intended number was sixteen, each of the frescoed bays would have had a tapestry beneath it, an arrangement which would have made better aesthetic and perhaps iconographic sense.

It is not known why the larger project, if such it was, was not completed, but there are various possible explanations, among them Raphael's other commitments. Not only was he completing the Stanza dell'Incendio di Borgo for Leo, but was also working, from August 1515, on a reconstruction of ancient Rome, again at Leo's request, while completing numerous commissions for private clients.[10] Financial considerations may also have played a part. Only two payments to Raphael are recorded for the cartoons, one on 15 June 1515, the other of 20 December 1516. The latter appears to mark the completion of the account.[11] There must, however, have been others, for the recorded payments total only 434 ducats whereas, according to Venetian diarist Marcantonio Michiel, Raphael was paid 1,000 ducats in all. When seven of the tapestries were displayed in the Chapel in late December 1519, Michiel noted: 'The designs for these tapestries for the Pope were made by Raphael of Urbino, an excellent painter, who received from the Pope one hundred ducats each, and the silk and gold in them are most abundant, and the weaving cost 1,500 ducats each, so that they cost in all, as the Pope himself said, 1,600 ducats apiece, though it was estimated and spread about that they were worth 2,000.'[12]

The richness of the tapestries was thus duly noted, and while Leo could always in theory justify such displays of magnificence as appropriate both to the place and to his role as Pope, it is possible that financial constraints held him back from following through a more ambitious project.

Leo's spending power and love of luxury were legendary and he was constantly in debt. Early in 1517, when the first of the tapestries was being woven, Leo was forced to embark on a war to regain the Duchy of Urbino from the della Rovere family; for this he had to borrow 800,000 ducats, more than the whole of the Papal annual income, so that times were hardly auspicious. On his death at midnight on 1 December 1521, Leo left the Papal treasury empty.[13] A marginal note, dated 17 December 1521, in the inventory of his tapestries, states that

8. Shearman, op. cit., p.42. This account is also discussed by Creighton Gilbert, op. cit., pp.537–40.

9. Shearman argues that seventeen would have been the ideal number, op. cit., pp.42–3. Creighton Gilbert convincingly refutes this, op. cit., p.539 and p.545.

10. For a general account of Raphael's career see R. Jones and N. Penny, *Raphael,* New Haven and London, 1983.

11. See V. Golzio, *Raffaello nei documenti, nelle testimonianze dei contemporanei e nella letteratura del suo secolo,* Vatican City, 1936, p.38 and p.51.

12. See John White, *The Raphael Cartoons,* HMSO, 1972, p.3. I have been unable to trace the original source of White's reference.

13. L. Pastor, *The History of the Popes from the close of the Middle Ages,* ed R. Kerr, vol.vii, London, 1923, pp.209–12.

the Raphaels were put in pawn after his death. According to Baldassare Castiglione, a prominent courtier and man of letters, this was in order to raise money for expenses such as those of the conclave, the body of cardinals assembled to elect the new Pope.[14] The tapestries were subsequently retrieved.

What Raphael brought to these subjects in terms of narrative design will be analysed later. Here the content of the scenes is summarized from the point of view of the congregation in the Sistine Chapel, which was wide-ranging, with a correspondingly varied theological expertise. Among the clergy who were permitted a place in front of the chancel-screen, in the area of the altar, were the College of Cardinals, Generals of the monastic and mendicant orders, patriarchs and visiting archbishops and bishops.[15] These were the most distinguished members of the congregation. Also included were the resident theologian, the sacristan, the majordomo of the Papal household, the chamberlain, secretaries, notaries and auditors. The laity included the Senators and Conservator of the City of Rome, visiting princes, the captain of the Swiss guard, servants of the cardinals, the choir, and the acolytes involved in performing the rites. Outside the chancel-screen were places for additional servants, pilgrims and spectators of substance. While none of the scenes represented in the tapestries individually posed great problems of interpretation, the full range of meanings inherent in the narrative cycle was complex and may only have been understood by certain members of this congregation.

In *The Miraculous Draught of Fishes*, Peter, the lowly and sinful fisherman is chosen by Christ to be the fisher of men and to take over the helm of the boat that represents the Church. In *Christ's Charge to Peter*, Raphael conflates two texts: in the first, taken from Matthew 16: 17–19, Christ appears to all the disciples after the Resurrection, and says to Peter 'I will give unto thee the keys of the Kingdom of Heaven'. In the second, Raphael draws on an incident from John 21: 15–17 when Christ appears to seven of the disciples only, and charges Peter to 'Feed my sheep', but without mentioning the keys. In the cartoon and tapestry, the two actions are made to occur simultaneously. The giving of the keys is seen as the fulfilment of Christ's earlier promise, while He commits to Peter the care of His flock.

There can be little doubt that the combination of these texts was designed to stress Peter's primacy among the apostles, which runs as a strong, if not exclusive theme throughout the cycle – there are more tapestries concerning Paul than Peter. The importance of the giving of the keys in this respect is underlined by the fact that the subject also appears in one of the fifteenth-century frescoes painted by Perugino.

14. Shearman, op. cit., p.140.

15. The chancel-screen or *cancellata* divided the chapel in two, and was originally further towards the altar than it is now. It separated the Pope and his entourage, who sat at the altar end, from less distinguished attendants.

A thematic parallel to *Christ's Charge to Peter* in the tapestries is provided by *The Conversion of Saul*, where Paul is appointed by divine revelation to be the teacher of the Gentiles.

The Healing of the Lame Man and *The Conversion of the Proconsul* were the first of Peter and Paul's miracles to be described in the Acts of the Apostles, and were performed among Jews and Gentiles respectively. In *The Death of Ananias*, Peter confronts the sins of the Jews, those of obstinacy and disobedience, while in *The Sacrifice at Lystra*, Paul confronts the Gentiles' sin of idolatry. There is thus a certain symmetry in these four scenes, which also stress the missions of Peter and Paul to their different peoples.

The tapestry of *The Stoning of Stephen* was almost certainly part of the Paul cycle. According to the Acts (7:58–60) it was Paul before his conversion, then named Saul, who took charge of the persecutors' garments during the stoning, consenting to Stephen's death. It therefore seems likely that it formed the beginning of the Paul cycle, coming before *The Conversion of Saul*. This view is strengthened by the fact that the landscape seems designed to continue from the one tapestry to the next. There is also a possible connection with *The Death of Ananias*, one side of which shows the distributions of the common goods to the people. It was for the purpose of distributing alms that the office of deacon was created, and Stephen was a holder of this office.

Slightly different in some ways is the scene of *Paul Preaching at Athens*, which it has been claimed was designed to hang outside the chancel-screen.[16] According to this view, its iconography was to be read in part as propaganda for the Pope and it was thus particularly suited to viewers outside his immediate circle. Its subject-matter does present a certain continuity with the other tapestries, particularly *The Sacrifice at Lystra* with its theme of conversion and idolatry, but also introduces other themes more specifically concerned with Leo's own interests. In addition to stressing the power of preaching, which Leo had personally taken steps to reform, the subject of Paul's sermon on this occasion was then thought to be the Resurrection, and the immortality of the body and soul. This was a matter on which Leo also had strong views, and on which he had issued a Bull confirmed at the eighth session of the Lateran council on 19 December 1513. Set before a temple of Mars in an imaginary Athens, the narrative may also allude to the Greek Academy recently established by Leo which led contemporaries to describe Rome as a new Athens on the Tiber. Behind the speaking Paul are portraits of Leo himself, the portly figure in the red cap, and the director of the Greek Academy, Janus Lascaris, standing behind him in a red robe.

16. Shearman, op. cit., pp.70–71.

14

Taken as a whole, the tapestry cycle focuses on the lementary roles and power of the two principal apostles. It complei. not only the decoration of the side walls but also that of Michelangelo's ceiling where Prophets and Sibyls elaborate on the parallel themes of revelation to the Jews and the Gentiles. In addition, there is an element of personal mythology woven into the scheme. The scenes of healing and conversion, the latter standing as a symbol of spiritual healing, can also be read as metaphorical allusions to Leo's aspiration to end schism and promote unity in the Church.

The personal relevance of the subject-matter is underlined by borders to the tapestries designed as fictive bronze bas-reliefs running below the narrative fields of the tapestries and showing scenes from Leo's religious and secular life. These were also designed by Raphael but the cartoons have been lost.[17] Leo's entry into Florence as Cardinal Giovanni de' Medici after his investiture in Fiesole in 1492 is represented below *The Stoning of Stephen*; his entry into Rome for the Conclave of 1513 and election to the Papacy below *The Miraculous Draught of Fishes*; the Sack of the Palazzo Medici and the flight of the Cardinal in 1494 below *Christ's Charge to Peter*, the capture of the Cardinal, then papal legate, at the Battle of Ravenna and his escape to Mantua in 1512 below *The Healing of the Lame Man*, and the recall of the Medici and their triumphant re-entry into Florence in 1512 beneath *The Death of Ananias*.[18] There were probably further events from the life of Paul beneath the tapestries representing his acts.

Other, vertical, borders for which the cartoons have again been lost, depicted *The Seven Liberal Arts*, *The Seven Virtues*, *The Hours*, *The Seasons, The Elements* and *The Labours of Hercules*, although the relationship of these to the central narratives is difficult to reconstruct with any certainty. These borders also survive in the tapestries in some cases.

The tapestries were not permanently on display but were put up on special occasions. Their intended hanging order has never been fully agreed and indeed there is no record that they were always hung in the same sequence. Other tapestry cycles were hung in a variety of ways, according, for example, to the liturgical occasion, a practice which was followed both by Sixtus IV and with the Scuola Nuova tapestries, commissioned either by Leo or by Clement VII.[19] It is possible that the Leonine tapestries were also hung in different ways at different times.

The most obvious order might seem to be to have Peter, with his special mission to the Jews, placed under Sixtus' fresco cycle of *The Life of Christ* on the left (our right) of the altar and Crucifix, and Paul,

17. For a discussion of the reliefs see Shearman, op. cit., pp.37–38 and pp.84–89.

18. Shearman, op. cit., p.37.

19. For the Scuola Nuova tapestries see *Raffaello in Vaticano*, Milan, 1984, pp.326–331, and D. Cordellier and B. Py, *Raphael, son atelier, ses copistes*, Paris, 1992, p.616.

apostle to the Gentiles, under *The Life of Moses* on the right (our left). However, this touched on a long-standing debate about the primacy and proper position of the two apostles, and there is ample evidence of an alternative tradition where Paul was placed on the left and Peter on the right.[20] The question is further complicated by the sheer diversity of meanings which can be extracted from the tapestries. This also means that a multiplicity of possible connections can be established with the frescoes above, and it is unwise to deduce a hanging order from an assumed relationship between them. The sequence of hanging of the tapestries is also problematic because of the question-mark over their intended number.

It is true that the tapestries vary in size, suggesting that they were designed for specific locations.[21] It also seems likely that a series of tapestries which formed part of such a carefully co-ordinated decorative scheme would be intended to have a particular order. There are also several features within the cartoons which appear to bear this out. Firstly, directional shadows suggest that Raphael took account of the light falling from the two windows that then existed in the altar wall – in *The Miraculous Draught of Fishes*, *Christ's Charge to Peter*, and *The Death of Ananias*, the light appears to come from the left while in the others it comes from the right.[22] Raphael must therefore have had a particular arrangement in mind in terms of which wall each tapestry was to hang on – although it is worth bearing in mind that this directional lighting may have been less apparent in the tapestries themselves – woven with gilt-silver thread and lit in part by candle and lamplight. There are also cases, such as that of *The Stoning of Stephen* and *The Conversion of Saul* where a certain sequence seems inevitable, and one might assume that the series would in general follow the order of the stories in the Bible. None of these factors is totally conclusive, however, and it is worth noting, as suggested above, that the intended order of the tapestry series may not have been followed in practice. Only in two cases does the intended order seem indisputable – that of *The Stoning of Stephen* and *The Conversion of Saul*, and *The Miraculous Draught of Fishes* and *Christ's Charge to Peter*. Here, the landscapes are designed to continue from one to the other, establishing these as adjacent pairs.[23]

The cartoons themselves have a long and complex history. Leo wanted the tapestries quickly: unwilling to wait until the set was completed, he had seven exhibited in the Chapel on 26 December 1519, to considerable critical acclaim. There is little doubt, then, that Raphael and his workshop had to work in haste, and the ten cartoons were completed in approximately a year.

20. On this see Shearman, op. cit., pp.38–41. Left and right in this case are taken from the viewpoint of the Crucifix and altar, not that of the spectator.

21. The stretching of the tapestries over time makes their fit in specific places hard to test with precision. The spaces on the altar wall which may have taken tapestries have also been covered up by Michelangelo's *Last Judgement*, painted between 1535 and 1541.

22. When Raphael designed the tapestries the altar wall carried the first two frescoes of the fifteenth-century cycle, with two windows above. The frescoes were covered over and the windows filled in when Michelangelo painted his *Last Judgement*.

23. The order of hanging adopted in the gallery at the V&A follows that proposed by John Shearman, which has been accepted by most scholars. The cartoons are, however, hung in reverse order, as they are reverse images of the tapestries.

There is little to indicate what Raphael's own attitude to the cartoons would have been but despite the speed at which they were executed they appear as remarkably finished objects. Raphael certainly would have been aware that the tapestries would constitute the only case where his work would be subject to direct comparison with that of Michelangelo, in his rival's painting of the Sistine Ceiling. The cartoons were also painted at a time when cartoons were becoming sought-after as objects in their own right and steps were sometimes taken to preserve them through the use of substitute or secondary cartoons. Other of Raphael's cartoons were certainly collected, as in the case of one for the painting of *St Michael* which was acquired by the Duke of Ferrara.[24]

Tapestry cartoons, however, presented something of a special case, at least those which, like Raphael's, were destined to be woven in the low-warp or *basse-lisse* technique. These were used in vertical strips by the weavers, suffering as a result varying degrees of damage and mutilation.[25] The weavers worked side by side with the strips of cartoon placed sideways beneath the warp threads of the loom, following the design with the coloured threads of the weft. The width of the strips was limited both by the size of the loom and by the arm-span of the weavers. The weavers worked on what was to become the back of the tapestry, producing a mirror-image of the cartoon, which therefore had to be designed in reverse. Yet as the Raphael cartoons and other examples, such as the *Fructus Belli* tapestry cartoons in the Louvre make clear, it was by no means impossible to reintegrate the strips to recover the complete image and their use in the weaving process did not always bar cartoons from being a desirable acquisition.[26]

There is in fact some evidence that, almost from the time of their inception, Raphael's tapestry cartoons were sought-after as works of art in their own right. Indeed, it is not out of the question that at some point Leo contemplated retaining the cartoons for himself, although tapestry cartoons most often became the property of the weavers. There are certainly known instances of patrons retaining tapestry cartoons. Prince Andrea Doria kept those for a set of tapestries of the *Furti di Giove* woven for him by Perino del Vaga in Flanders in about 1532–35, for his palace in Genoa.[27] Inventories of 1606 and 1620 listed 'forty-six pieces of painted paper, one missing, with the stories of the said tapestries of the *Furti di Giove*', the number of pieces suggesting that the sections had not yet been reassembled after the weaving process. By 1630, the Duke of Mantua had acquired from Charles I one of *The Triumph of Scipio* tapestry cartoons designed by Giulio Romano for François I of France in the 1530s, the object returning to the British Royal Collection in 1786, when it was purchased from Richard Cosway.[28] Even more to the point,

24. Golzio, op. cit., pp.74–5.

25. For a recent account of the low-warp weaving technique see A. Cavallo, *Medieval Tapestries in the Metropolitan Museum, New York*, New York, 1993, pp.18–25.

26. On the *Fructus Belli* cartoons see G. Delmarcel et al., *Autour des Fructus Belli: une tapisserie de Bruxelles du XVI siècle*, Paris, 1992.

27. See B. Davidson, 'The *Furti di Giove* Tapestries designed by Perino del Vaga for Andrea Doria', *Art Bulletin*, September 1988, vol.LXX, no.3, pp.424–449.

28. See *François 1er et ses artistes: dans les collections du Louvre*, Paris, 1982, p.120. Charles I acquired the Mantuan collections for the British Royal Collection, but they were sold off after his death. The cartoon is now in the Louvre.

Fig.2. Maiolica dish with
scene of *The Healing of
the Lame Man* from a print
after Raphael's cartoon,
*c.*1540–50
Pesaro ware, diam. 38cm
Victoria and Albert Museum,
London, Salting Bequest
C.2251-1910

29. Shearman's version of the history
of the cartoons during the rest of the
sixteenth century has recently been
questioned by Tom Campbell in
'School of Raphael tapestries in the
collection of Henry VIII', *Burlington
Magazine*, vol.CXXXVIII, no.115,
February 1996, pp.69–79. I am
indebted to Campbell's article for
much of what follows.

30. See D. Landau and P. Parshall, *The
Renaissance Print: 1470–1550*, New
Haven and London, 1994, pp.119–68.

by 1521, Cardinal Domenico Grimani had acquired Raphael's cartoon
of *The Conversion of Saul* for his private collection in Venice, giving
some indication of the fame the Raphael cartoons had acquired.

By early in 1517, Raphael's cartoons were despatched to Brussels
for weaving in the workshop of Pieter van Aelst, foremost supplier of
tapestry to the Habsburg rulers of the Low Countries. Brussels, rather
than an Italian centre would have been chosen because it was the most
revered centre of tapestry production, from both the technical and
aesthetic points of view. The first weaving was finished by 1520–21 after
which no further sets of tapestries appear to have been made from the
cartoons in van Aelst's workshop.

The subsequent fate of the cartoons themselves is obscure.[29] Their
designs, however, had an immediate, wide and long-lasting impact. The
popularity of the compositions is testified to by the fact that they were
engraved very early in their history, the earliest print dating from 1516.[30]
During the sixteenth century numerous prints after them are recorded
and their making was encouraged by Raphael through his collaboration
with the engraver Marcantonio Raimondi. The first prints were made

Fig.3. Martial Courteys
Enamel platter with *The Death
of Ananias* from a print after
Raphael's cartoon, *c.*1580
Limoges enamel, 40.6 x 54.9cm
Los Angeles County Museum,
gift of Varya and Hans Cohn

from Raphael's preliminary drawings, the finished cartoons being in-accessible in Brussels. Thereafter prints after the cartoons were made and copied, and images from them used to adorn objects in a wide variety of media, such as maiolica plates (fig.2) and Limoges platters (fig.3). Piecing together the history of the cartoons themselves is, how-ever, not easy. It is known that a set of tapestries to their design was woven before 1534 for François I, probably in the Brussels workshop of Willem Dermoyen. These have since been destroyed and it is not known if they were made from the original cartoons or from copies, although the former seems more likely. Van Aelst probably passed on the car-toons, with the possible exception of *Paul in Prison*, a narrow strip of cartoon which does not seem to have been used again after the first weaving, and *The Conversion of Saul*, already with Cardinal Grimani, which must have been replaced by a copy.

The next set of tapestries is probably that made for Henry VIII by an unknown Brussels workshop around 1540; these are presumed to have been destroyed in 1945 but are known from photographs. Given the importance of the patron, it seems likely that the original cartoons were used, and it is interesting to note that the landscape in *Christ's Charge to Peter* in this set is altered in the same way as that in the Leonine set.[31]

In the 1540s or 1550s, the cartoons appear to have passed to the workshop of another Brussels weaver, Jan van Tiegen, who made one set now in Madrid, probably for Charles V or Philip II of Spain, and another which was acquired by Cardinal Ercole Gonzaga, now in Mantua. In these sets, however, the landscapes in *Christ's Charge to Peter* follow faithfully that of Raphael's cartoon.

While it is possible that all these sets were made from copies, there is no reason why this should have been the case. By the second half of the century the original cartoons had almost certainly been used more than once, because a group of letters, written in 1573 from Brussels to Cardinal Granvelle, who had expressed interest in a set of tapestries after them, related that they were far too damaged for further use and that sets were then being made from copies.[32] The careful pricking of the cartoons makes clear that at least one set of copies was made, and it is likely that there were others.[33] The Granvelle letters also confirm that the cartoons were still in Brussels in 1573, although their exact whereabouts is not known.

It is interesting to speculate on the significance that the tapestries held for the different patrons of the tapestry sets, given the specific nature of their original iconography. Famed as objects of particular luxury and magnificence, their authorship by Raphael must also have made them of interest to any prospective collector. Once removed from the context of the Sistine Chapel, and divested, as they would have been, of the borders relating to Leo X, their function as a statement of the primacy of St Peter and of the Pope, would have been somewhat diluted. Even with the omission of *Paul in Prison*, there were more tapestries devoted to Paul and Stephen together than to Peter, and it seems likely that they came to be seen simply as exemplary renderings of certain acts of the apostles.

By 1623 the cartoons were in Genoa from where seven were obtained by Charles, then Prince of Wales, for the sum of £300.[34] Francis Crane, manager of the Mortlake tapestry works set up by James I in 1619, using Flemish immigrant weavers, was instrumental in their acquisition.[35] It was primarily the tapestries that interested Charles. He would have been familiar with the set woven for Henry VIII, which remained in the Royal Collection until after Charles's death, and an admiration for these may have played a part in his desire to commission a set of his own. He may have had little thought of the cartoons becoming valued as independent works of art although it is interesting

31. For a discussion of this alteration see pp.58–59 below.

32. Shearman, op. cit., p.145.

33. The pricking of the cartoons is discussed on pp.57–60 below.

34. Charles did not acquire *The Stoning of Stephen*, and it is not known when it was separated from the remaining eight. David Howarth has, however, found some evidence that both this and *The Conversion of Saul* were in the collection of Cosimo II de' Medici by 1627. See D. Howarth, 'William Trumbull and Art Collecting in Jacobean England', *The British Library Journal*, vol.20, no.2, Autumn 1984, pp.155–8.

35. See W.G. Thomson, *A History of Tapestry from the Earliest Times until the Present Day*, 2nd ed., London, 1930, pp.278–82.

36. For a discussion of this point see pp.54–56 below.

Fig.4. Transmitted-light photograph of part of *The Conversion of the Proconsul*. This detail reveals the initials CR, referring to Charles I, which are stamped on the back of each strip of this cartoon

to note that transmitted-light photographs of *The Conversion of the Proconsul* reveal the initials CR stamped on the back of each strip, perhaps suggesting that he took some pride in their possession (fig.4).

Charles's tapestries were not woven from the original cartoons but from copies made by Francis Cleyn, who was also commissioned to design new borders. It is not entirely clear how Cleyn made his copies,[36] but the Mortlake sets are among the most faithful to the cartoons of the tapestries now existing, suggesting that the copies were precise. Two more sets of painted copies were also made during the reign of Charles I. It is therefore likely that the strips were at some point temporarily reassembled for this purpose.

After the death of Charles I, the original cartoons were reputedly kept, still in strips, in wooden boxes in the Banqueting House at Whitehall. Interestingly, however, and for reasons which are not entirely clear, they were included among the goods reserved from sale for the service of the State during the period of the Commonwealth. It is possible that Cromwell envisaged them being used again at Mortlake at some point – he and his supporters were also lovers of fine tapestry.[37] On the other hand they were valued at no more than their purchase price of £300 and may have been considered not worth selling. A *Madonna and Child with Saints*, then attributed to Raphael, and later known as *La Perla* was valued at £2,000 and sold to Philip IV of Spain. The cartoons were also valued at considerably less than the £1,000 placed on Mantegna's *Triumphs of Caesar*, likewise retained by the Commonwealth, which were spoken of periodically as potential cartoons for tapestry although they were never intended for this purpose.

At the Restoration the cartoons returned to the possession of Charles II and an unsuccessful attempt was made to buy them for the Gobelins factory in France at the instigation of Louis XIV. Charles II himself appears to have had little interest in the cartoons and, according to the art critic Jonathan Richardson the Younger, was only dissuaded from selling them by his treasurer, the Earl of Danby.[38] In 1680, he pawned them to a William Hewer for the sum of £3,000, in part to pay for the making of other pieces of tapestry by his own tapestry maker, Francis Poyntz. The proviso that, while in Hewer's security, they should not be 'embezzled or copied by or for anybody's use', suggested, however, that their status had risen and they were clearly also recognized by now as a financial asset.[39]

It was on the accession of William III in 1688 that the fate and the status of the cartoons began to undergo a change. There are several reports of the cartoons having been exhibited during his reign, almost certainly with the strips again temporarily reintegrated, both at Whitehall, and at the Tower, on the latter occasion for the purpose of making painted copies.[40] It was not until the late 1690s, however, that the cartoons began to acquire something of the status they enjoy today, when William III ordered the painter Henry Cooke and the surveyor Parry Walton permanently to reassemble the strips in which the cartoons remained. He also ordered Sir Christopher Wren to set aside space for them in his ongoing remodelling of Hampton Court Palace, in the redesigned King's Gallery.

By the end of 1699, the cartoons were installed in this specially designed gallery, set in wooden panelling high above eye-level, framed as independent works of art, in an arrangement which is clear from the frontispiece to Simon Gribelin's engravings of the cartoons (fig. 5). It is apparent from this that little attention was paid to the subject-matter of the cartoons, which were hung with an eye to formal pattern rather than in any notional series. Care was, however, taken for their preservation, with a fire-proof barrier constructed between the gallery and the

37. Shearman, op. cit., p.147, and Thomson, op. cit., p.295.

38. Shearman, op. cit., p.147.

39. PRO 52/8 King's Warrant Book VIII (pp.218–221 and 222). I am most grateful to my colleague Wendy Hefford for this reference.

40. Shearman, op. cit., pp.148–49.

The Seven Famous Cartons of Raphael Urbn Drawn at the Command of Pope Leo the 10.th as Patterns for Tapestry: They were bought by K. Charles the first (at the Persuasion of S.r P. P. Rubens) and brought from Flanders into England: afterwards K. William fix'd them in his Palace of Hampton Court in the Gallery here Represented. In 1707 they were drawn and Engraven by Sim: Gribelin and by him most humbly Dedicated to Her Late Majesty

SEMPER EADEM
ANNA REGINA.

Septem Tabulas Chartaceæ (Iussu Leonis X Pontificis Romani) a Raphaele Urbinate in Aulæorum Texturam pictæ quas Rex Carolus I. (Suasu P.P. Rubens Equitis) ex Flandriâ in Angliam advehi jussit. et quas postea Rex Gulielmus Palatio suo Hampton-Court dicto. in Pinacotheca hic representata collocavit. Anno 1707. eas delineavit Erique incidit Sim. Gribelin et Seren.mæ Annæ Reginæ humilissime Dedicavit.

S.G. inv. a sculp.t & excudit. 1720

Fig. 5. Simon Gribelin
Frontispiece to engravings of
Raphael cartoons, 1720
British Museum, London

apartments above, and a fire kept lit in winter to reduce humidity in the gallery. The cartoons were also covered with green silk curtains, not visible in Gribelin's engraving, to protect them from the effects of light.

The reassembly of the cartoons was clearly a formidable task, and the difficulties which it presented to Cooke and Walton are still visible in their condition today. A great deal of patching was required, the cartoons having suffered extensive damage through the process of being cut into strips and through years of subsequent usage and neglect. Cooke and Walton glued the strips onto a layer of coarse canvas, still visible at the back of the cartoons, a process which in itself was problematic as the strips expanded differently under the impact of the glue. The surfaces of the cartoons show evidence of extensive creasing,

23

wrinkling and distortion caused by their attempts to force the strips down flat.

Inevitably, during this process, the strips were in some cases misaligned, and there are numerous instances where the design does not match neatly either side of the join. One of the most conspicuous occurs in *Christ's Charge to Peter*, where the two halves of the domed building on the horizon are noticeably out of line with each other (fig.6). Lower down this cut the configuration of feet and drapery of the apostles has been significantly distorted and clumsily rectified, the original outlines being readily traceable by following the prick marks which were used to make early copies of the cartoons. The losses along the joins have been made good with extensive use of filler, then overpainted. Other cases of overpainting occur where the paper surface of the cartoon had been entirely lost, as in *The Death of Ananias*, where the face of the man on the right in the blue hat has been repainted onto bare canvas underneath.

Another significant case of repainting occurs in *Christ's Charge to Peter*, in the sky and horizon, to which an additional strip was added, where white overpainting obscured many details, including the statuary on the building in the centre. In several instances, notably *The Healing of the Lame Man* and *The Conversion of the Proconsul* the cartoons were also cropped and trimmed to enable them to fit into the spaces designed for them at Hampton Court, entailing slight losses of detail at the edges. Similar losses occur at the points of the joins between strips in *The Death of Ananias* and *Christ's Charge to Peter*.

The purely aesthetic arrangement of the cartoons at Hampton Court marked something of a watershed in their status, for it is clear from this that their subject-matter was not their only point of interest. From this point on, due in no small part to the writings of the Richardsons, art critics and connoisseurs, the cartoons became canonical, not only because of their subject-matter, but as masterpieces of the art of narrative, or history painting, which the Richardsons were prepared to rank above the Raphael Stanze in this respect, despite having never seen the latter. In an essay in *The Connoisseur* of 1725, they wrote: 'But whatever our number [of pictures], or variety of good pictures is, we have the best history pictures that are anywhere now in being, for we have the cartoons of Raphael at Hampton Court, which are generally allowed even by foreigners, and those of our own nation who are the most bigotted to Italy, or France, to be the best of that master, as he is incontestably the best of all those whose works remain in the world.' The combination of display of the cartoons at Hampton Court and the writings of the Richardsons brought the cartoons into the

Fig.6. Detail of *Christ's Charge to Peter*. The domed building in the background was cut through by the weavers and the two parts misaligned when the strips were reassembled. Heavy white overpainting obscures some details of other buildings

public consciousness in an unprecedented way. There was no doubt a great deal of national pride involved in the Richardsons' writings – as John Shearman has observed, 'It was in this period that the first steps were taken towards the installation ... of Raphael as an honorary Englishman'.[41]

This sense of Raphael, and specifically of the cartoons, as national treasures is illustrated by a complaint lodged by John Wilkes in the House of Commons in 1777. It occurs in the context of his urging George III to support the purchase of more printed books and paintings:

> Such an important acquisition as the Houghton
> Collection, would in some degree alleviate the concern,
> which every man of taste now feels at being deprived of
> those prodigies of art, the Cartoons of the divine Raphael.
> King William, though a Dutchman, really loved and
> understood the polite arts. He had the fine feelings of a

41. Shearman, op. cit., p.151.

man of taste, as well as the sentiments of a hero. He built the princely suite of apartments at Hampton Court, on purpose for the reception of those heavenly guests. The English nation were then admitted to the rapturous enjoyment of their beauties. They have remained there until this reign. At present they are perishing in a late baronet's smoky house at the end of a great smoky town… Can there be, Sir, a greater mortification to any English gentleman of taste, than to be thus deprived of feasting his delighted view with what he most desired, and had always considered as the pride of our island, as an invaluable national treasure, as a common blessing, not as private property.[42]

Thus, while in the tradition of academic criticism the cartoons remained exemplars of the art of history painting on a grand scale, they also came to be looked upon as essential elements in the formation of taste and required viewing for any cultivated gentleman.

The house referred to by Wilkes was Buckingham House (now Buckingham Palace) home of the late Sir Charles Sheffield, bought by George III for Queen Charlotte in 1761, to which the cartoons had been moved in 1763. It is clear from contemporary reports that opportunities to see the cartoons at Buckingham House were rare, and after a brief period of movement around different rooms at Windsor, George III ordered their return to the Wren Gallery at Hampton Court.[43] They were then hung in a different order from that formulated under William III, one which may better have reflected Raphael's intentions for their organization.

The fortunes of the cartoons did not end there. Between 1816 and 1819 they were brought to London for exhibition at the British Institution, and in 1823 *Christ's Charge to Peter* was loaned for copying to Somerset House, then home to the Royal Academy and its schools. Copying, in fact, was allowed of all the cartoons, as they increasingly became seen as a school for art students – particularly for their rich repertoire of gestures and expressions – a practice which has continued until relatively recent times. Richard Redgrave, Surveyor of the Royal Collections from 1857 to 1879, commented adversely on the practice of allowing tracings with hard pencil to be made of the cartoons, and evidence of this process is still visible in the cartoons today.[44] Clusters of small pin-holes, often concentrated around heads and hands, testify to the fixing of tracing paper to the surface of the cartoons to allow copies of salient features to be made. Redgrave also commented on the adverse

42. Shearman, op cit., p.152.

43. It may have been at this point that the cartoons were provided with the ornate 'Maratta' frames in which they are still displayed. It is also possible, however, that this occurred on their move to Buckingham House. There is conflicting evidence in this respect, on which see Shearman, op. cit., pp.154–5.

44. Shearman, op. cit., p.155.

conditions caused by the constant risk of fire at Hampton Court, from damp, and from the dust of 200,000 visitors who walked though Wren's Gallery each year.

The undeniably popular display of the cartoons at Hampton Court was thus not considered unproblematic and the debate about their appropriate location arose again in 1824 on the foundation of the National Gallery, then housed in Pall Mall. In April 1833, appealing once again to the notion of the cartoons as national treasures, Benjamin Robert Haydon wrote an open letter to the Prime Minister, Lord Grey, arguing for a new building which would be large enough to house the cartoons, for, he asked, 'Will any gallery which excludes the cartoons of Andrea Mantegna and Raffael be a National Gallery?'[45] In 1836, a distinguished group of connoisseurs and artists was summoned to give evidence before a Select Committee of the House of Commons and asked to express a view upon the appropriate fate of the cartoons. Opinion was generally in favour of their installation in a new National Gallery building. As *The Art-Union* asked in an editorial of 15 September 1839, continuing the theme of the cartoons as exemplars of high style, 'Why are they allowed to moulder on the walls of Hampton Court useless and unproductive in their effects, when, if removed to the National Gallery, they would produce better results upon Art than the Elgin Marbles?'[46]

The removal of the cartoons to Trafalgar Square was not to be. After the death of Prince Albert in 1861 his eldest daughter Victoria, then Crown Princess of Prussia, proposed that the cartoons be transferred on loan to the South Kensington Museum, now the Victoria and Albert Museum, in fulfilment of her father's expressed wish to bring together 'all Raphael's works now existing in England'. It is not entirely clear why the new National Gallery was not to be the destination for the loan, since Queen Victoria had given the Gallery, at the Prince's request, a number of his earlier Italian paintings, as well as some German and early Netherlandish works. The trustees made a last-minute application for the loan, but the transfer to South Kensington was approved by Queen Victoria on 16 March 1865, since which date the cartoons have remained on loan to the Museum.

The implementation of the Prince Consort's plan for the cartoons is not without interest, for it suggests that his view of the function of these works was to be educational as well as elevating and as documents in the history of art. It certainly took little heed, as Redgrave may have wished, of their original function as designs, for they were hung together with miscellaneous copies of other works by Raphael, in a range of different media. A full-size eighteenth-century copy of Raphael's

45. Shearman, op. cit., p.156.
46. Ibid.

27

Transfiguration was hung with them, together with a tapestry of *Christ's Charge to Peter*. In addition there were drawings after the Stanze frescoes, small copies of them in oil, as well as sixteen lunettes and some grotesque pilasters copied from Raphael's Loggia, and a Gobelins tapestry after a *Holy Family* in the Louvre. In 1883, to mark the fourth centenary of Raphael's birth, three full-size copies were commissioned of the missing tapestry designs, to be made from the tapestries in Rome, which were then hung with the collection. It was not until 1950 that the cartoons were hung alone in the present gallery, in conditions more closely approximating those that the tapestries would have enjoyed in the Sistine Chapel, regaining their full status both as great works of art and as objects of design.

In 1964–5 a campaign of cleaning and discreet restoration was undertaken, including some pastel retouchings.[47] The recent campaign of work on the cartoons has been largely non-interventive, and was prompted by the need for building refurbishment as much as conservation needs, as well as the desire to display the cartoons with purpose-designed lighting. Taking into consideration the many vicissitudes through which they have passed, the cartoons remain in remarkably sound condition, although they are undeniably fragile. No attempt has been made to remove past retouchings or restorations, most of which are in any case visible to the naked eye, not least because these, too, form part of the cartoons' fascinating history. Loose flakes of paper on the surface have been reattached and the damaged edges rebound with specially dyed Japanese paper. Where necessary the backing canvas has been gently cleaned using a very light vacuuming technique. Our aim at this stage is not materially to interfere with the fabric of these magnificent objects but to discover as much as we can about them with the aid of new investigative technologies, as well as creating the optimum conditions for the enjoyment of these exceptional works of art.

47. There is no full published account of the 1960s restoration. Some aspects of the sampling of pigments were published by J. Plesters, 'Raphael's Cartoons for the Vatican Tapestries: A Brief Report on the Materials, Technique and Condition', *The Princeton Raphael Symposium. Science in the Service of Art History*, ed. J. Shearman and M. Hall, Princeton, 1990, pp. 111–24.

THE CARTOONS

Fig.7. Raphael, *The Miraculous Draught of Fishes*, 1515–16
Bodycolour on paper mounted onto canvas (tapestry cartoon), 3.2 x 3.9m
Victoria and Albert Museum, London

Fig. 8. Raphael, *Christ's Charge to Peter*, 1515–16
Bodycolour on paper mounted onto canvas (tapestry cartoon), 3.4 x 5.3m
Victoria and Albert Museum, London

31

Fig. 9. Raphael, *The Healing of the Lame Man*, 1515–16
Bodycolour on paper mounted onto canvas (tapestry cartoon), 3.4 x 5.4m
Victoria and Albert Museum, London

Fig. 10. Raphael, *The Death of Ananias*, 1515–16
Bodycolour on paper mounted onto canvas (tapestry cartoon), 3.4 x 5.3m
Victoria and Albert Museum, London

Fig.11. Raphael, *The Conversion of the Proconsul*, 1515–16
Bodycolour on paper mounted onto canvas (tapestry cartoon), 3.4 x 4.5m
Victoria and Albert Museum, London

34

Fig.12. Raphael, *The Sacrifice at Lystra*, 1515–16
Bodycolour on paper mounted onto canvas (tapestry cartoon), 3.5 x 5.6m
Victoria and Albert Museum, London

Fig.13. Raphael, *Paul Preaching at Athens*, 1515–16
Bodycolour on paper mounted onto canvas (tapestry cartoon), 3.4 × 4.4m
Victoria and Albert Museum, London

THE TAPESTRIES

Fig.14.
Christ's Charge to Peter
Tapestry, 4.9 x 6.4m
with borders
Vatican Museums,
Rome

Fig. 15.
*Paul Preaching
at Athens*
Tapestry, 4.9 x 5.2m
with borders
Vatican Museums,
Rome

Fig. 16.
The Sacrifice at Lystra
Tapestry, 4.9 x 5.8m
with borders
Vatican Museums,
Rome

Fig.17.
The Healing
of the Lame Man
Tapestry, 4.9 x 5.7m
with borders
Vatican Museums,
Rome

Fig. 18.
The Miraculous
Draught of Fishes
Tapestry, 4.9 x 4.4m
Vatican Museums,
Rome

L·SERGIVS·PAVLVS
ASIAE·PROCOS:
CHRISTIANAM·FIDEM
AMPLECTITVR·
SAVLI·PREDICATIONE

2

Structure,
Technique and Usage

ONE of the most fascinating questions to arise from the study of the cartoons is that of how Raphael went about constructing these immense paper objects. It must have been a formidable technical challenge, and the way in which Raphael approached the task provides some insight into how he perceived the cartoons.

There is comparatively little historical data on which to draw when discussing cartoons of any type. The Raphael cartoons form the first set of tapestry cartoons on paper known to have survived, so that there are no earlier examples which might assist in interpreting or analysing Raphael's working methods. Moreover, in many ways the Raphael cartoons are considered to be something of a watershed in cartoon design, and it is thus important to exercise caution in speaking of them as typical in any way. Other examples which do survive, such as the *Fructus Belli* cartoons in the Louvre, the *modelli* for which were probably provided by Giulio Romano in the mid 1540s, and *The Triumph of Scipio* cartoons in a private collection, also designed by Giulio in the early 1530s, postdate the Raphael tapestry cartoons by a number of years, and should therefore be treated carefully in helping us to understand how Raphael went about this momentous project.[1]

Sixteenth-century technical treatises, such as the technical prefaces to Giorgio Vasari's *Lives of the Artists* of 1550 and 1568, the most

1. For the *Fructus Belli* cartoons see Delmarcel, op. cit. For the *Triumph of Scipio* series see E.H. Gombrich et al., *Giulio Romano*, Milan, 1989, pp.467–9. A few earlier painted cloths survive which may have been intended as cartoons for high-warp tapestry.

important source of information on sixteenth-century artistic practice, and Giovan Battista Armenini's *On the True Precepts of Painting* of 1586, provide relatively little information about the actual physical construction of cartoons although they do stress that cartoons had begun to be considered as objects of some value in their own right and recommend procedures for preserving the precious originals.[2]

Vasari does not discuss cartoons for tapestry in his technical prefaces but writing on fresco cartoons he explains that these were executed on a vertical surface:

> Cartoons are made thus: sheets of paper, I mean square sheets, are fastened together with paste of flour and water cooked on the fire. They are then attached to the wall by this paste, which is spread two fingers' breadth all round on the side next to the wall, and are damped all over by sprinkling cold water on them. In this moist state they are stretched so that the creases are smoothed out in the drying. Then when they are dry the artist proceeds, with a long rod, having a piece of charcoal at the end, to transfer to the cartoon…all that in the small drawing is shown on the small scale.[3]

Fresco cartoons probably offer the closest comparison to those for tapestry and as well as Vasari's writing we have a little information about the making of three well-known examples, all carried out before the Raphael tapestry cartoons.

In 1503 and 1504 respectively, Leonardo and Michelangelo were each commissioned to execute a monumental battle fresco for the *Sala del Gran Consiglio* in the Palazzo Vecchio in Florence, *The Battle of Anghiari* and *The Battle of Cascina*. Both of these required large cartoons. The surviving evidence suggests that the artists made elaborate provision for the preparation of these vast paper works. Leonardo, for example, had special blinds made for the windows of the room provided for him in Santa Maria Novella which may have been intended to achieve the quality of light that he required while also reducing draughts.[4] He also constructed an elaborate scaffolding, described by Vasari as '*uno edifizio artificiosissimo*', from which to work, which could be increased in height by drawing the parts together or rendered wider by being lowered. Although the exact nature and function of this apparatus are still a matter of some dispute it seems likely that Leonardo wished to work with the cartoon placed at the same height as the fresco, rather than at ground level, so that he could judge the final effect as carefully as possible.[5]

2. On this and other aspects of cartoons see the works cited at notes 8 and 9 below. See also E. Borsook, 'Technical Innovation and the Development of Raphael's Style in Rome', *Canadian Art Review*, vol.12, part 2, 1985, pp.127–36, and L. Wolk-Simon, 'Fame, *Paragone* and the Cartoon', *Master Drawings*, vol.30, no.1, 1992, pp.61–82.

3. *Vasari on Technique*, trans. L. Maclehose, ed. G. Baldwin Brown, New York, 1960, p.213.

4. G. Gaye, *Carteggio inedito d'artisti dei secoli XIV, XV, XVI*, 3 vols, Florence, 1839–40, vol.II, pp.88–90.

5. For a discussion of this device see M. Hirst, 'I disegni di Michelangelo per la *Battaglia di Cascina*' in E. Borsook and Fiorella Superbi Gioffredi eds., *Tecnica e Stile: esempi di pittura murale del Rinascimento italiano*, 2 vols., Milan, 1986, vol.1, pp.43–58.

Especially interesting is the fact that both Leonardo and Michelangelo employed specialist *cartolai* or paper-makers, Giovandomenico di Filippo and Bernardo di Salvadore respectively, to cut and flatten the sheets of paper, and that both were quite well-paid for the task.[6] Michelangelo also used his *cartolaio* to paste together the numerous sheets of paper that made up his cartoon. Neither artist relied on his own *garzoni*, young studio assistants, for these particular tasks, preferring to employ specialists. It would be unwise to make too much of this, for the artists and their workshops may simply have been too busy not to delegate this laborious work. Nonetheless, taken with other evidence, it does suggest that a certain care went into the making of preliminary designs. This implies that even at this stage artists did not envisage them being cut up and used directly for transfer onto the *intonaco*, or wet plaster, of the wall. Such was the value placed on some artists' cartoons that it was not unusual for their outlines to be pricked through onto secondary cartoons to be cut up and used on the walls, as recommended by Armenini, so that the original could be retained.[7] There was also, of course, a practical reason for the use of secondary cartoons, since the original image could then act as a guide to the artist when painting.

The size of paper used by Michelangelo for his cartoon, the *foglio reale bolognese*, which measured 44.5 x 61.5cm, was frequently used by artists constructing large paper objects. This larger size reduced the effort of joining together numerous sheets of paper. As has been stated in a recent discussion of cartoons, 'Large cartoons were most commonly drawn in black chalk or charcoal…on relatively thin paper, usually in the *reale* size. Large cartoons were assembled from multiple sheets glued together side by side with overlapping borders.'[8]

This also applies to the fragment of cartoon by Michelangelo for his *Crucifixion of St Peter* fresco in the Pauline Chapel, Rome, completed in 1550. The cartoon fragment, now in the Museo Capodimonte, Naples, is made up of thirty *fogli reali bolognesi* pasted together. While we cannot know exactly how, or by what procedure the sheets were assembled, transmitted-light photographs of the cartoon fragment show a fairly neat grid of sheets glued together in a regular fashion.[9]

Raphael himself was not a complete stranger to the making of large cartoons. He used cartoons of different kinds for the frescoes in the Stanze in Rome, and recent research has shown how varied and inventive he was in his use of preparatory designs.[10] His cartoon for the lower part of *The School of Athens* fresco in the Stanza della Segnatura in Rome, painted for Julius II in about 1510, survives in the Ambrosiana, Milan, and shows the main figural composition without the architectural background (fig.21).[11] The whole measures 2.75 x 7.95m and

6. For Michelangelo's use of a *cartolaio* see Hirst, op. cit., p.46. For Leonardo see Karl Frey, *Studien Zu Michelagniolo Buonaroti und zur seiner Zeit, Jahrbuch der Koniglich Preussischen Kunstsammlungen*, XXX, 1909, p.129. I am grateful to Carmen Bambach for this reference. Paper often came folded into quires (24 sheets), and the folds required flattening out, although the creases resulting from the folding would not have been substantial. I am grateful to Peter Bower for discussing early paper with me.

7. G.B. Armenini, *On the True Precepts of Painting* (1586), ed. E Olszewski, Burt Franklin and Co., 1977, p.174.

8. See *Master Drawings*, vol.30, no.1, 1992, p.3.

9. See C. Bambach, 'Michelangelo's Cartoon for the *Crucifixion of St Peter* Reconsidered', *Master Drawings*, vol.XXV, no.2, March 1988, pp.131–141.

10. I am grateful to Arnold Nesselrath for discussing this with me.

11. See K. Oberhuber, *Il cartone per la Scuola di Atene*, Milan, 1972.

Fig.21. Raphael
The School of Athens
(cartoon for the lower part of
the fresco), *c.*1510
Black chalk and charcoal,
2.75 x 7.95m
Pinacoteca Ambrosiana,
Milan

is made up of 195 sheets each measuring 40 x 28cm, pasted together in eight rectangular groups. The cartoon is rendered in heavy *chiaroscuro*, and was not itself used to transfer the design to the *intonaco*. The outlines have been pricked through to make secondary cartoons for use on the wall, as discussed above. The original would then have served as a guide to the painter in organizing the fresco's complex masses of light and shade. However, while these examples provide useful comparative information, and demonstrate the care with which some artists approached the making of cartoons for fresco, there are two essential differences between these and the tapestry cartoons.

First, the cartoons discussed above were probably not destined to be cut up and used, or subjected to the exigencies of direct use in the fresco process, let alone those of the weaving process. Second, and perhaps most important, all were executed largely in dry media such as chalk or charcoal, less likely to put a strain on the paper surface than the body-colour used by Raphael in the tapestry cartoons. Vasari's account

of the making of cartoons reflects this bias towards fresco as he describes them being executed in charcoal.[12]

The Raphael cartoons differ not only because they were to be cut up and used on the weavers' looms but also because they are painted. While in some places the paint appears slightly transparent, generally speaking it is relatively thick and opaque. The paint would have made the large paper surfaces quite heavy and hard to handle, while the wetness of the medium may have increased the risk of tearing. Nor is there any doubt that the complete surfaces were assembled before painting began, as the paint uniformly goes over the overlaps between the individual sheets.

Given these considerations it is perhaps not surprising that the construction of the tapestry cartoons is extremely sound and, for the most part, carefully carried out. For one thing, the sheets of paper used are relatively small, measuring on average 28 x 42cm. They are also very regular in size, to the extent that any radical departure from these

12. Cartoons for panel paintings could also be executed in charcoal but these are not the subject of Vasari's discussion.

dimensions usually signals a feature such as a repair, a patch or an inset of some kind, expanding the width of the sheet from edge to edge. In the case of *The Death of Ananias*, for example, a sheet measuring 44.5cm across was found to have an odd fragment of cartoon inserted into it as a form of repair, thus increasing its width.

There are, of course, some other irregularities in the sheet size. In *The Conversion of the Proconsul*, for example, a few very small sheets, measuring 13cm wide, are inserted into the pattern, perhaps indicating that some remnants of paper needed to be used up. A desire to save paper may also explain the changes in the direction of the paper from portrait to landscape format, that occur in some cases towards the edges of the cartoons. This, and the appearance of 'left-overs' from time to time may indicate that, unlike Michelangelo, Raphael did not employ a specialist *cartolaio*, but left the making up to his assistants. There are certainly subtle variations in the construction of each cartoon which might indicate different members of the workshop at work, as well as the fact that some were carried out in greater haste. The construction of *The Healing of the Lame Man*, for example, is noticeably less tidy than that of the other cartoons and also includes some contemporary patches and repairs; taken together with the sometimes sketchy quality of the painting and underdrawing, this might suggest that the whole was carried out rather hurriedly, and was possibly one of the last to be done.

The size of the sheets used by Raphael suggests that they are half sheets, probably of the *reale* size. Although there are no clearly identifiable creases or signs of folds which might indicate the size used, rope marks – patterns of tiny wrinkles – have been identified along the long edges of some sheets. Such marks resulted from the hanging of the paper to dry over hair ropes during the making, and roughly indicate the centre of the sheet; their presence in the cartoons would seem to confirm that they are made up of half sheets. Since the cartoons are backed onto canvas, and the paint is quite thick, it has not proved possible to locate a watermark which might help identify the supplier that Raphael used for his paper.

The use of small sheets in the cartoons may initially seem surprising since it might be thought to make the construction of such large surfaces unnecessarily time-consuming. However, by using small sheets and increasing the number of joins, thus doubling the thickness of the paper at frequent intervals, and increasing the amount of glue present, Raphael strengthened the surface as a whole. In this way he could compensate for the stress put on the paper surface by the application of paint. He may also have preferred the relative manageability and ease of

Fig.22. Transmitted-light photograph of *Christ's Charge to Peter*
The grid of dark lines seen in this detail indicates the overlaps between the sheets of paper making up the cartoon, and shows the regularity of its construction

handling of smaller sheets, as opposed to the full-size *fogli reali*, since he used sheets of similar dimensions in the Ambrosiana cartoon.

The sheets themselves are pasted together in a regular and orderly way, with the overlaps being relatively, if not completely consistent in width. The overlaps are also generally consistent in width from end to end, and it seems that Raphael and his assistants worked carefully and methodically, avoiding any irregularity or unevenness of construction that might put stresses or strains on the paper surface. Transmitted-light photographs, taken with flashlights from behind the cartoon, show an even, almost geometric grid of sheets of regular size, making up the whole (fig.22). It is also interesting that there are no deckle edges – the rough edges that resulted from the process of paper-making – visible in the cartoons. All the sheets have been trimmed, suggesting that Raphael was aiming for a smooth, flat surface on which to paint, avoiding the cockling caused by the deckle edges. In other words, his concerns may have been aesthetic as well as structural or purely practical, going beyond what was strictly necessary if the cartoons were thought of simply as designs for weaving which would then be discarded.

The question remains open as to exactly how Raphael went about constructing the cartoons, and particularly how he supported wet paper of this size. There is no doubt that the cartoons were painted on a vertical surface, since the paint drips visible in the X-rays all run downwards.[13] It may be that Raphael did use Vasari's method, fixing the cartoon to a wall with an outer rim of paste, and relying on the strength of the medium thick paper, the soundness of the overall construction, and a painting medium which was not too watery, to prevent the sheets from tearing or unsticking. It is worthwhile noting, however, that Vasari's method was not always reliable. Humidity could be a problem, for example, and in June 1505, in his Madrid notebook, Leonardo wrote that while he was painting his *Battle of Anghiari* fresco, heavy rain caused his cartoon to tear while on the wall.[14]

The measurements of the sheets of paper, and of the overlaps between them, have been determined in two ways in the recent research campaign. The first is hand measurement, carried out completely on *The Death of Ananias*, and in the form of random sampling on the remaining cartoons. This has been combined with a pioneering use of the technique of photogrammetry, which had never been used on works of this kind and which is most often employed for aerial mapping or the spatial measurement of buildings.[15] The technique involves the taking of two photographs of an object at different angles from each other which, when superimposed and viewed through a monitor, give a three-dimensional picture of the image. Variations in relief can then be mapped and measured by computer. Since the overlap between two sheets of paper produces a change in the relief configuration of the cartoon, the sizes of the sheets can also be measured and recorded in this way, to an accuracy of plus or minus two millimetres. Not only is this technique labour-saving and accurate, it is also highly desirable from a conservation point of view, since it does not involve direct contact with the cartoon. A degree of verification by eye is, however, required to ensure that the monitor is not reading creases in the cartoons, which also cause differences in relief, as paper overlaps.

Examination of the structure of the cartoons is, in fact, uniquely difficult. This is both because of their size and fragility, and because they remain backed onto the coarse canvas applied by Cooke and Walton when they reintegrated the strips in the 1690s. Not only, therefore, are the cartoons opaque but what might be significant information may be hidden between the painted sheets and the canvas. Were we able to see

13. We are grateful to Howard Pearson of A.T. Roffey & Co. Ltd, for undertaking the complex task of X-raying the cartoons, and to Agfa-Gavaert Ltd, for providing the film and assisting with development. Agfa-Gavaert Ltd and Stone Foundries Ltd also kindly assisted with processing the X-rays.

14. Leonardo da Vinci, *The Madrid Codices*, ed. L. Reti, National Library of Madrid, McGraw-Hill Book Co. (U.K.) Ltd., 1974, vol.V, p.2.

15. We are extremely grateful to Plowman Craven and Associates for undertaking the photogrammetry of the cartoons.

Fig.23. Transmitted-light photograph of *Christ's Charge to Peter*
The web of fine lines visible across the whole of the photograph indicates the canvas onto which the cartoon strips were laid in the late seventeenth century. The dark patches of different sizes indicate paper repairs to the cartoon applied at various points in its history

the back of the sheets with the joins unconcealed by paint layers, we might, for example, gain a better idea of whether Raphael had re-used old sheets, perhaps containing discarded sketches or notes of different kinds, or whether he used new paper. Many sheets show holes in the corners, now patched from behind with tiny pieces of paper, suggesting that they may have been used before and pinned to a drawing-board. Lastly, where there are several layers of patching on the back of the paper, as made visible by transmitted light, we might be able to place them in chronological order, relating each to a specific campaign of restoration.

Considerable information has, however, been gleaned by the use of a number of investigative techniques, as well as by close scrutiny with the naked eye. Transmitted-light photography has been particularly useful in furthering understanding of the structure of the cartoons, providing a view through the object as a whole, and showing up patches, pin-holes and areas of different density (fig.23). Raking-light photography has contributed to the 'mapping' of the surface of the cartoons and enabled the recording of major distortions, as in the top right of *The Death of Ananias*, where the paper and canvas support have begun to sag (fig.24).

Fig.24. Raking-light photograph of *The Death of Ananias*
Raking-light photographs show clearly distortions in the structure of a cartoon, such as the bulge in the top right-hand corner

We have thus been able to establish conclusively that the original cartoons consisted of only one layer of paper sheets, backed onto the seventeenth-century canvas used by Cooke and Walton. Transmitted-light photographs, such as that of *Paul Preaching at Athens* (fig.25), have also revealed another layer of canvas in certain areas, mainly around the edges, and around the places where the cartoons had been cut for the weavers, areas which show up darker in the photographs. This canvas is also visible from the front of the cartoon, in places where the paper surface has been lost, and is finer and lighter than the overall backing canvas (fig.26). The presence of these canvas layers or strips is confirmed by raking-light photography, where the ragged edge of each strip is visible as an uneven raised line to either side of each cut (fig.27). X-rays also reveal the torn fibres of these strips at certain points.

Careful examination of the outside edges of the cartoons in these areas reveals that these are strips of canvas, each of around 8–9cm wide, which have been glued to the back of the paper as a form of re-inforcement of the damaged edges of the strips. On one side, the canvas generally extends for a number of centimetres beyond the edge of the paper, while on the other, the edges of the paper and the canvas are flush with each other. This indicates that the two edges were designed to over-

Fig.25. Transmitted-light photograph of *Paul Preaching at Athens*
The shadowy areas around the edges of the image and in vertical bands down the front reveal the presence of the canvas strip-linings applied probably in the first half of the seventeenth century. The grey area in the bottom left-hand corner is probably the result of heavy overpainting

16. These holes are different from those which show up as point of bright light on the transmitted-light photographs, which relate to the pinning of tracing paper on the surface of the cartoons for the purpose of making copies.

lap, as is still generally the case. Almost invariably, the edges without the protection of the extra canvas extension have sustained considerably more damage and loss.

The most likely explanation of this feature is that the canvas strips were rough reinforcements applied in the seventeenth century, both to strengthen the cartoon strips and to enable them to be temporarily rejoined. Not only were the canvas strips designed to overlap each other but it is also possible to detect pin-holes running up the side of where the join must have come. These generally occur in the corners of sheets which are the strongest points because of the added thickness of the paper caused by the overlaps.[16]

The cartoon strips were exhibited at Hampton Court and the Tower during the late seventeenth century, and they would also have had to be reintegrated in some way to allow Francis Cleyn to make his copies for Mortlake in the 1620s. It seems most likely that the canvas strips or strip-linings are linked to these episodes in the cartoons'

Fig.26. Macrophotograph of area from *The Death of Ananias*
The cut made in the cartoon by the weavers is clearly visible in this detail. It is also possible to detect the two canvases – inside the cut area the dark, coarse layer applied by Cooke and Walton, and to the left the finer, lighter layer of the earlier strip-lining

history. Carbon dating locates the canvas with 99 per cent certainty to between 1390 and 1640, which is not inconsistent with this theory. The likelihood is that the cartoons were then mounted on temporary stretchers, and some of them show holes around their outside edges, consistent with their having been prepared in this way.

When Cooke and Walton came to rejoin the strips on a permanent basis at the end of the seventeenth century, they had to contend with these strip-linings of canvas, and it is interesting to note that, for reasons unknown, they dealt with them differently in each cartoon. In the case of *Christ's Charge to Peter* and *The Death of Ananias*, and to a lesser extent in *The Miraculous Draught of Fishes*, they were meticulously trimmed and cut back and the excess canvas removed. The paper edges were also trimmed so that the cartoon strips could be neatly abutted. In *The Conversion of the Proconsul* and *Paul Preaching at Athens*, however, the canvas strips were left as they were and the cartoon strips pulled together. The excess canvas was then overlapped, usually bunching up in the process. The joins were then overpainted, with results which are aesthetically much less pleasing.

The original cutting of the cartoons into strips was also done with varying degrees of finesse, although it is not entirely certain whether Raphael or the weavers carried it out. The fact that the cartoon strips vary dramatically in width, from between 41cm to 66cm is curious, and may indicate an exchange of views between the two parties. Generally speaking, the weavers would try to avoid cutting a cartoon through a head or other crucial area where a specialist weaver might be employed. The craftsmen who wove faces were different from those who specialized in landscape, and were also paid more for their work. It would thus make sense to avoid using their labour on two strips, wasting time on the change, if it could be confined to one.

However, in both *Christ's Charge to Peter* and *The Death of Ananias*, the cuts barely manage to avoid the faces, cutting through hair, ears, or the corner of an eye. On the other hand, in *The Conversion of the Proconsul* a particularly narrow strip appears to have been designed specifically to avoid cutting through a figure. These variations may suggest that Raphael cut the cartoons and that, while attempting to do so in compliance with the weavers' requirements, and remaining within a maximum width, he may not have fully understood the technical issues at stake. It is also possible that, at the weavers' request, he modified his approach as work went on, attempting to avoid figures where possible. It may also be, however, that weavers cut the cartoons, and that Raphael's dense figural style simply made it impossible for them to avoid cutting the cartoons through heads in some cases, or dividing them up unevenly.

Fig.27. Raking-light photograph of *The Conversion of the Proconsul*
On either side of each vertical cut in the cartoon, it is possible to detect the ragged edge of the canvas strip-lining appearing as a slightly raised line

On balance it seems more likely that the weavers did the cutting, and there is some evidence that the cartoons were transported to Brussels whole. All manifest long, relatively straight vertical creases running down the length of the surface at intervals suggesting that they were transported rolled, as was customarily done with carpets and tapestries, or folded. The creases, which are not easy to account for otherwise, probably result from them having been slightly compressed while in this state. It is almost certain that they occurred while the cartoons were still complete pieces since, once cut up, the vertical strips would have been rolled or folded horizontally.

That the cartoons have been extensively pricked also sheds light on their history. This process has nothing to do with their use in weaving, but is probably linked to the making of copies. It is certainly hard to explain in any other way, and recent examination has confirmed that the pricking holes go right through the original layer of paper. The pricking is not uniform, suggesting that numerous different artisans were involved in this time-consuming process. In some areas the outlines have been pricked densely and with great care, in others it is looser and less meticulous, while some details have not been pricked at all. Nevertheless, with the notable exception of the landscape background in *Christ's Charge to Peter*, almost all the outlines of the cartoons have been pricked around. Close examination reveals, however, that, with the exception of one column in *The Healing of the Lame Man*, they were only pricked once. The number of surviving tapestry-sets after the cartoons suggests, however, that several sets of copies were made, presumably by other means.

It is impossible to date this pricking process precisely. It certainly pre-dates the seventeenth-century strip-linings, as the pricking does not go through the canvas. Furthermore, when Cooke and Walton rejoined the cartoon strips, misalignments occurred between them which also occur in the pricked lines; the latter must therefore have been made before the reassembly. One suggestion is that the pricking was carried out in the workshop of Pieter van Aelst, and that the resulting copies rather than the valuable originals were used on the looms for the weaving of the Leonine tapestries.[17] This is, however, difficult to reconcile with the fact that the originals have been cut for weaving, admittedly at an uncertain date. It also seems likely that, given the importance of the commission, the originals would have been used, however highly prized the cartoons were in their own time. From Leo X's point of view the most important thing was the tapestries themselves, and he would have wanted the weaving to be as faithful and accurate as possible. The most likely scenario is that Pieter van Aelst, after using the cartoons in strips, sold them, with the exception of *The Conversion of Saul*, which had been bought by Cardinal Grimani, and which he must have replaced by a copy. The fact that in the subsequent known sets made in sixteenth-century Brussels, this tapestry is of inferior quality to the others, supports the notion that the others were made from the originals.[18] At the same time, the pricking would have been easier to carry out while the cartoons were still whole, which might again link it to van Aelst's workshop.

There is one, mysterious factor which might support the idea that the pricking had to do with the weaving of Leo's tapestries. In *Christ's Charge to Peter* the main figural group has been carefully cut around so as to separate it from the landscape (fig.28). The cut abruptly severs the heads of the apostles from the horizon above, including some parts of their haloes. The figure of Christ has also been cut around, separating him from Peter, and above their heads, the two figures with their flock of sheep have been similarly cut.[19]

17. C. Bambach, *The tradition of pouncing drawings in the Italian Renaissance workshop: Innovation and derivation*, Ph.D. Dissertation, 2 vols, Yale University, 1988, pp.369–70.

18. Shearman, op. cit., pp.144–5. It is possible that copies made by van Aelst, or later weavers, travelled outside Brussels.

19. It could be that this simply represents a different way of dividing the cartoon up for weaving, using a process rather like that of *giornate*, or patches of plaster in fresco painting. However, there would then have been no need to cut the cartoon into strips.

Fig. 28. Detail of *Christ's Charge to Peter*
This cartoon has been cut around the figural group for the convenience of the weavers enabling them to separate the figures from the landscape. The line of the incision is clearly visible above the apostles' heads

20. On this see p.20 above. The cartoon probably remained in sections until after the tapestry-set made for Henry VIII, since here the landscape is altered in a similar way.

The function of these cuts was almost certainly to enable the weavers to work on the figures and the landscape separately, by separating the parts of the cartoon. In Raphael's design the heads and the landscape are almost inextricable, which would have made difficult the co-operation of two specialists weaving heads and detailed landscapes. In the weaving, therefore, they moved them apart, inserting a plain grassy band between the heads and the buildings. They also improvised in other areas of the landscape, altering and adding details, for it was in the execution of landscape that they generally exercised the greatest freedom in their work.

In view of these alterations, it is interesting that the pricking of the cartoon stops abruptly at the point at which it has been cut above the heads, and that there is no pricking in the landscape. This might suggest that the pricking was in some way related to this weaving and was thus carried out in Pieter van Aelst's workshop. It is also possible, however, that the cartoon remained cut into sections when van Aelst passed it on, and that it was pricked at a later date, sometime before the letters of Cardinal Granvelle in 1573 at which point we know that copies were in use.[20] The absence of pricking in the landscape may reflect this division

59

into sections but it is equally likely that weavers' workshops found Raphael's complex, *sfumato* background too difficult and labour-intensive to prick, and that they preferred to copy it more loosely.

Other, less complex landscape backgrounds in the cartoons are certainly pricked. In *The Conversion of the Proconsul*, for instance, where the background and figures do not overlap, both sides of the landscape are pricked, while in *The Death of Ananias*, a row of prickmarks in the landscape in the top right-hand corner allows us to reconstruct the profile of a row of buildings which has been lost from the painting itself. In *The Miraculous Draught of Fishes* all but one of the features of the landscape have been meticulously pricked, including the now faint horizon line and some of the lines of the waves in the sea.[21]

A final reflection on the pricking of the cartoons concerns the area of the inscription beneath the throne in *The Conversion of the Proconsul*. Transmitted-light photography shows that this area has been extensively patched, but the patching took place before the pricking. The letters themselves have been very densely pricked, causing some of them to lift. In these areas we can see prick-marks on the patching material, together with some writing which, although impossible to date precisely, is not inconsistent with the mid-sixteenth to early seventeenth century. This patching is interesting because it was carried out before the copying, suggesting that the copyists were concerned to protect in advance an area which would have to be heavily worked.

The detail of this inscription also suggests that Raphael's own attitude to the cartoons was not purely pragmatic. As John Shearman has observed, unlike the rest of the cartoon, the inscription is not rendered in reverse. This would seem to suggest that Raphael wished the cartoon to be legible as an independent entity. In this respect, as in the depiction of landscape, the integrity of the cartoon took precedence over the convenience of the weavers.[22]

Raphael's approach to the painting and drawing of the cartoons bears this out. The medium used is a mixture of pigments, water and animal glue. It has a relatively high proportion of binder to pigment.[23] In most places the paint is quite thick and opaque although the charcoal underdrawing is sometimes visible through the paint layers.

While some underdrawing is thus visible to the naked eye, infra-red reflectography has revealed a great deal that is not otherwise apparent. Perhaps the most striking discovery has been the fact that, while substantial underdrawing exists, it is nowhere near as detailed or extensive as one might expect in works on such a grand scale and with such complex compositions – nor does it reveal extensive or significant *pentimenti*. There is certainly no trace of squaring up, or other means by

21. The leafy tree at the extreme right edge of the landscape background remains mysteriously unpricked.

22. This observation was first made by Shearman, op. cit., pp.136–7.

23. On this see Plesters, op. cit., pp.114ff.

Fig.29. Detail of *The Conversion of the Proconsul*

which the artist might have translated his small preparatory drawings onto the larger surface. For the most part, the drawing appears remarkably spontaneous and direct, and suggests an extraordinary confidence and assurance.

Not surprisingly, the most detailed underdrawing appears in *The Miraculous Draught of Fishes*. Here, the poses of the figures and the foreshortenings involved are particularly complex, and the drawing reveals Raphael trying out and refining the position of each limb, and the location of the figures in space. In the landscape, as in that in *Christ's Charge to Peter*, Raphael does not draw the forms in any detail but sketches in the outlines of their shapes, searching for a rhythm and an overall balance of domed buildings and spires, towers and hills.

In other cartoons, the figures are less well-defined through underdrawing than in *The Miraculous Draught of Fishes*. The rudiments of the figures are drawn in but little more, except where difficult foreshortening is involved, as in the figure of the dying Ananias. Even complex architectural structures are only rendered in part, with the emphasis on establishing the orthogonals of the perspective and the positions of the basic components. The drawing also varies in quality from one cartoon to the next which might reflect the intervention of different hands or the speed of execution of each one. In *The Miraculous Draught of Fishes* the underdrawing is light and free, and extremely dynamic, as well as defining the forms in detail. In *The Healing of the Lame Man* it is often quite crude and approximate, especially on the figures. Interestingly, however, the drawing of the columns is extremely refined.[24]

The cartoons also appear to have been painted with remarkable freedom and assurance despite their relatively finished appearance. That is not to say that they are sketchily rendered since, for the most part, the paint is applied with care and notable attention to detail. Indeed, one of the most striking aspects of the cartoons' appearance is the combination of broad, free painting, for example in areas of drapery, with careful, meticulous and detailed handling, as in areas of decoration, footwear, and landscape and, of course, in the painting of heads. In *The Death of Ananias*, for example, the drapery of the apostles is painted with broad sweeps of thickish paint. By contrast, the two female figures to the left of the composition have elaborate decoration on their garments, while their headdresses are created by leaving the bare paper to stand for tone, enlivened by a few strokes of reddish paint. In *The Conversion of the Proconsul*, the near sleeve of Elymas appears to have no pigment on it at all, but only a brown glaze, or a layer of medium, thickly applied, which has soaked into the paper to give a yellowish shadow (fig.29). The multi-coloured garment of the cripple in the *Sacrifice at Lystra*, although damaged by water, is a particularly rich and complex example of Raphael's painting technique, combining thickish green and yellow pigments with areas of bare paper, white highlights and thin brown and yellow glazes. By contrast, in *The Miraculous Draught of Fishes*, simply by using azurite in different degrees of saturation, mixed here and there with lead white, Raphael succeeds in rendering the shifting blues of the sea and sky, the dusky blue of distant buildings, the glassy blue surface of the calm water, and the different blues of the garments worn by Christ and Peter. In other instances one can see Raphael approaching the painting of the cartoons much as he would have done his contemporary fresco commissions, especially in the delicate hatching of heads and faces such as that of the startled woman in *The Death of Ananias*. Similarly, Raphael's concern for the perfection of his nudes is apparent in the dense and meticulous cross-hatching and parallel shading which he used to paint the fishermen in *The Miraculous Draught of Fishes*.

24. The relationship between the underdrawing and the preparatory drawings for the cartoons will be the subject of a later study.

The variety of painting techniques employed in the cartoons, their inventiveness and the overall sophistication of handling are remarkable. To some extent the variety of techniques can be accounted for by the presence of different hands in the execution of the cartoons, something which is also clearly apparent in the widely differing range of physiognomies. It may also reflect the relative speed at which each one was painted as well as himself working in different ways and experimenting with different techniques.

All this shows that Raphael worked up the cartoons to a level beyond what was strictly necessary for the weavers. This is true not only of the detail he applied to them, and the extent of his *chiaroscuro*, but also to the thickness of his paint and the range of colours used. The little surviving evidence suggests that, prior to Raphael, the designer of a tapestry cartoon generally gave the weavers little more than colour indications, sometimes in the form of washes or scumbles of colour, sometimes in the form of written instructions.[25] While designers would ensure that the colour was iconographically correct, they probably did little more than this, leaving the choice and distribution of colour to the experience of the weavers whose job it was to construct a decorative ensemble. It seems unlikely that cartoons before these by Raphael were painted in full colour, partly because the weavers were the acknowledged experts in the choice and matching of shades. In addition, as we shall see, with their own range of dyes, the weavers would rarely have been able to match exactly the colours that a painter would have used in bodycolour. The main function of the cartoon was to provide the lineaments of the composition and the rest was left to the discretion of the weavers. In the wake of the Raphael cartoons, however, fully coloured cartoons appear to have become increasingly the norm, the situation escalating until weavers at the Gobelins factory in the eighteenth century complained that their artistic freedom was being curtailed and that they were being reduced to mere copyists for cartoon designers.[26]

Further evidence to support the proposition that the colour used by Raphael was unusual is Vasari's description of the cartoons as *cartoni coloriti*.[27] He also noted that Leonardo da Vinci designed a tapestry cartoon for the King of Portugal showing *The Original Sin*, rendered in *chiaroscuro*.[28] Furthermore, the *Fructus Belli* cartoons, while coloured, are rendered with thin washes of colour, of a limited range, distributed across the surface in a schematic and decorative way, rather than being modelled in colour in the manner of the Raphaels. The closest analogy to the Raphaels is probably presented by the fragments of the Scuola Nuova cartoons, designed by Giulio Romano and assistants for either Leo X or for Clement VII, which show evidence of vivid colour, and *The*

25. On this see inter al. J. Coffinet, *Arachne ou l'art de la tapisserie*, Geneva, 1971, pp.39–56; J. Jobé, ed., *The Art of Tapestry*, London, 1965, pp.32–4 and M. Ferrero Viale, *Arazzi Italiani del Cinquecento*, 2nd ed., Milan, 1982, pp.8–9.

26. Thomson, p.447.

27. Giorgio Vasari, *Le Vite de' Più Eccellenti Pittori, Scultori ed Architettori*, ed. G. Milanesi, Florence, 9 vols, 1878, vol.IV, p.370.

28. Vasari, op. cit., vol.IV, p.23.

Triumph of Scipio cartoons, but this may simply reflect Giulio's experience of working with Raphael.

It is difficult to know how to interpret this evidence. It would perhaps be over-simplistic to take it as a sign that Raphael wished the cartoons to be considered as independent paintings. It could simply be that he made little distinction between these and his other large-scale commissions in terms of colour and technique. Yet this in itself may not be without its significance, for it suggests that his approach to the commission was not entirely pragmatic. If Raphael did not change his technique to suit the needs of tapestry designs it at least suggests that he did not wish anything to leave his workshop that did not conform to the highest standards of his painterly art.

3

Design and Colour

Leo X's choice of Raphael to design the tapestry cartoons must reflect in part the fact that, by the time of the commission, the artist was already acclaimed as a master of dramatic narrative and design. His talent in this respect had been amply proven in a number of previous commissions, particularly his frescoes for the Stanze, a suite of apartments in the Vatican which he had begun to decorate for Pope Julius II in 1508 and was just completing for Leo, with the help of his assistants, at the time of the tapestry commission (fig. 30). Raphael's ability to combine a variety of narrative interest with dramatic impact was clearly demonstrated in these frescoes by the way in which he subtly united diverse groups of figures around a central dramatic point. These qualities are also evident to some degree in the tapestry cartoons. At the same time there are qualities of design in the cartoons which are distinctive, and which reflect Raphael's response to the different challenges posed by the commission. This chapter will examine the qualities of design in the cartoons, including their use of colour, in order to gain a better understanding of how Raphael interpreted his task.

Discussing the design of the cartoons is inevitably a difficult matter, partly because the hanging order of the tapestries, if there was only one, cannot be established beyond doubt.[1] Thus, while it might seem natural to assume that the design of each cartoon was partly calculated

1. For a discussion of this point see pp. 15–16 above.

to take into account the physical position of the corresponding tapestry in the Chapel, this is something which cannot be taken for granted.

Likewise, the order in which the cartoons were executed, or the degree of participation of Raphael's assistants – foremost among whom would have been Giulio Romano, Gian Francesco Penni and Giovanni da Udine – cannot be conclusively established. For this reason, discussions based on the notion of a chronological evolution of style or the participation of different hands are fraught with problems and are therefore dealt with only briefly in the following pages.

It is certainly true that even the relatively inexperienced eye will notice differences in both style and quality between the cartoons. There is a marked difference in quality, for example, between the figures of the apostles in *Christ's Charge to Peter* and those in *The Death of Ananias*, and few scholars would hesitate in attributing the whole of *Christ's Charge to Peter* as well as *The Miraculous Draught of Fishes* to Raphael

Fig.30. Raphael
The School of Athens, c.1510
Fresco
Stanza della Segnatura,
Vatican, Rome

Fig.31. Detail of *The Healing of the Lame Man*

himself, with the possible exception of the flora and fauna in the latter. Since the publication of Vasari's *Lives of the Artists*, these have traditionally been attributed to Giovanni da Udine, for although Vasari does not claim specifically that Giovanni painted these parts, he states that Raphael used him as a specialist for this kind of work. When discussing Giovanni's participation in painting the still-life elements in Raphael's altarpiece of *The Ecstasy of St Cecilia*, Vasari wrote: '…he [Giovanni], brought his manner herein to so close a similitude with that of Raphael, that the whole work appears to have been executed by one hand', a statement that illustrates one of the problems posed by attributing parts of the cartoons, and the extent to which artists could assimilate each others' styles.[2] It is also probable that much of the marbled architecture and flooring in the cartoons, such as that in *The Conversion of the Proconsul*, was executed by Gian Francesco Penni since he was a specialist in this kind of work.

The complexity of attribution is not simply related to the fact that the artists working on the cartoons must to some degree have absorbed and emulated each others' styles, consciously or not. It is also

2. Vasari, op. cit., vol.VI, p.551.

Fig. 32. Detail of *The Healing of the Lame Man*

evident that, even where it is detectable with any certainty, the apparent division of labour in the cartoons sometimes appears contrary to what one would expect. In *The Sacrifice at Lystra*, there does appear to be some logic in the distribution of work. The main figures – those of the two saints, the man with the ram on the left, the executioner and the cripple – are most certainly by Raphael. The other figures are notably inferior in quality, although even here there are variations between them, while the landscape in this case is too formulaic to attribute to the master. In *The Death of Ananias*, however, the situation is less simple. Not surprisingly, Raphael appears to have executed the key figure of Ananias. Yet the figure of the recoiling woman in the foreground, less crucial to the composition, also shows a hatching technique in the face characteristic of Raphael's work in fresco. However, the almost caricatural and much more prominent figure of the man beside her seems much closer to the style of Giulio Romano. In *The Healing of the Lame Man*, the heads of the two

Fig.33. Detail of *Paul Preaching at Athens*

cripples are probably by Raphael, but the figures of the apostles seem too crude to attribute to his hand, particularly that of Peter – even taking into account the effects of later retouching (fig.31). However, the exquisite figure of the woman on the right, and that of her baby, are beautifully painted and confidently modelled, and appear to be Raphael's own work (fig.32). In *The Conversion of the Proconsul*, Paul and Barnabas both appear to be by Raphael, as does the blinded Elymas. However, the central figure of the Proconsul, while strong in conception, is relatively weak in execution, as are the figures on the right. And yet, the less significant figure of the Proconsul's attendant on the left, standing on the steps, while slightly rubbed, is very finely painted and even now retains some of its initial strength in the head.

In *Paul Preaching at Athens*, the majority of the figures are of a quality and consistency which enable us to ascribe them to Raphael, although he almost certainly delegated some of the painting of drapery and architecture. The main anomaly is the pair of slightly over-sized figures in the right foreground, almost certainly attributable to Giulio Romano, who do not seem to fit in position or scale into the composition as a whole (fig.33). Although they play a key role in the Bible story, since they were said to have been converted by Paul's speech, they appear here as something of a compositional afterthought. It is perhaps revealing that visible on the woman's clothing are letters reading *S. Paul predict* (fig.34) This may indicate that they also seemed odd to the weavers, who labelled the strip so as to be sure to which tapestry it belonged. It seems that Raphael did not always restrict himself to key figures, as one might have expected.

It is important to remember that the tapestries had to fit into an already rich and complex scheme of decoration in the Sistine Chapel.

Fig.34. Detail of *Paul Preaching at Athens*

Fig.35. View of the interior of the Sistine Chapel, Rome, looking towards the altar. The tapestries were hung in the Chapel to mark Raphael Year in 1983, at the height for which they were originally intended

Hanging just above eye-level on the lower walls of the Chapel, above the stone benches provided for its occupants and below the fifteenth-century frescoes, they had to compete with and complement a scheme of decoration which was already very intricate and which, most important for Raphael, included Michelangelo's ceiling frescoes (fig.35).

One salient fact of which Raphael had to take account was that the framing elements of the existing decoration were extremely decorative and highly illusionistic. The fifteenth-century frescoes, for example, are separated from each other by fictive, decorative pillars, painted as if in relief and adorned with antique motifs, made to look as if they were supporting an entablature. In addition, each fresco has two kinds of inner frame, which create the illusion that they are views through a window (fig.36). On the ceiling above, Michelangelo's frescoes are set in an architectural framework of unprecedented complexity, including fictive bronze figures, medallions and illusionistic *all'antica* architecture, all of which was taken as a display of the artist's virtuosity (fig.39).

Raphael responded by giving each tapestry an illusionistic frame-work made up of a number of elements. As discussed earlier, not all of these were purely decorative since some played a part in the political and thematic function of the tapestries. However, Raphael added to these a greek-key motif in blue along the bottom, and a running guilloche (braided bands) motif surrounding the whole narrative field. Also, at the sides of the tapestries, lining up with the fictive pilasters dividing the fifteenth-century frescoes, he included borders composed of antique and grotesque motifs which referred liberally to Michelangelo's lively nudes. In these respects, the tapestries blended in to an extent with the existing decoration of the Chapel, and the framing elements undoubtedly added to the overall richness of the objects.

That is not to say, however, that these devices did not present Raphael with something of a conflict. They unquestionably diminish the illusionistic quality of the central field of his designs, and the directness

Fig.36.
Domenico Ghirlandaio
The Calling of the Apostles,
1481–82
Fresco
Sistine Chapel, Rome

Fig. 37. Giulio Romano
*The Battle for the Milvian
Bridge*, 1519–21
Fresco
Sala di Costantino, Vatican,
Rome

of the relationship between the spectator and the central narrative, making us aware of them as images enclosed within a decorative frame, identified, as it were, with the surface of the wall. The scenes are presented as framed pictures rather than as immediate incidents appearing before our eyes. For this reason, the experience of the tapestries is both less direct and less dramatic than that of the cartoons themselves, as now seen without their borders.

There can be little doubt that Raphael wanted the spectator's experience of the narratives to be both direct and involved. The perspective in the cartoons of *Paul Preaching at Athens* and *The Death of Ananias*, for example, is carefully calculated in relation to the spectator's eye-level, so that we feel ourselves directly engaged with the stricken Ananias, or feel part of the foreground participants in the crowd around Paul. At the same time, in each cartoon, Raphael attempts to convey a convincing illusion of space to draw the spectator into the image, although in contrast to his frescoes in the Stanze, the degree of recession is not usually very deep. Thus, to some extent Raphael seems to have taken account of the fact that tapestries conventionally concentrated on surface pattern, and it is fascinating to compare the cartoons with the fresco of *The Battle for the Milvian Bridge*, painted by Giulio Romano in the Sala di Costantino, around 1519–21, almost certainly to Raphael's design (fig.37). The fresco is envisaged as a fictive tapestry, with fringed borders and edges painted as if curling away from the wall. Here, there is much less spatial recession, the figures being arranged in a frieze-like manner along the surface of the wall revealing the artist's awareness of tapestry compositions.

There are signs that Raphael attempted to compensate for the lack of directness and for the loss of clarity created by the weaving medium. In many cases, his figures appear excessive in scale, and their gestures unnaturally exaggerated. While this may have been a deliberate feature of style, a kind of hyperbole which makes the cartoons into the visual equivalent of passionately delivered sermons, it may also have been partly his attempt to preserve in the tapestries the clarity and directness of the cartoons.[3]

An equal preoccupation for Raphael would certainly have been the comparison that would be made between the tapestries and Michelangelo's frescoes, esteemed particularly for the vigour and dynamic qualities of their figures and their complex poses. On the one hand, Raphael's response seems clear-cut, in the monumentality of his figures enveloped in large swathes of drapery. A particular case in point is his figure of Christ in *Christ's Charge to Peter*. While the beautiful *sfumato* head reflects the influence of Leonardo, the muscularity and power of this figure, created through extensive use of light and shade, reflect an acute awareness of Michelangelo's work; indeed, Christ's commanding gesture, with His outstretched arms, echoes in reverse the imperious gesture of Michelangelo's *God creating the Sun and Moon* in the ceiling fresco above (fig.38). In *The Miraculous Draught of Fishes* the mirrored poses of the muscular apostles hauling in fish pay tribute to the paired figures of Michelangelo's seated nudes on the ceiling, while also referring to his struggling figures in *The Battle of Cascina* cartoon. In *The Sacrifice at Lystra*, the scene on the left of the cartoon showing the presentation of a ram has clear parallels with Michelangelo's *Sacrifice of Noah* above (fig.39). On the other hand, in at least two of the cartoons, *Christ's Charge to Peter* and *The Miraculous Draught of Fishes*, Raphael exploited to the full his talent for creating landscapes of breathtaking beauty, the one area in which Michelangelo's art was often said to be deficient, and which were the same time designed to harmonize with the

3. The connection between Raphael's pictorial style and contemporary rhetoric is discussed by Shearman, *Only Connect*, Ch.V.

Fig.38. Michelangelo
God creating the Sun and Moon, 1511–12
Fresco
Sistine Chapel ceiling, Rome

landscape backgrounds of the fifteenth-century frescoes above. These landscapes show clearly Raphael's delight in virtuoso effects, as he captures details such as the drifting smoke in *The Miraculous Draught of Fishes*, the light dancing on the trees, the diffused rosy glow of the sunlit buildings, and the delicate arcs of the birds overhead.

To make these comparisons is in no way to denigrate Raphael's achievement or originality. Indeed quotations from other, revered works of art were both expected and valued in contemporary painting. The point is rather that the design of the cartoons took place within a highly competitive artistic environment, one to which Raphael had to respond with the added knowledge that the weaving process could minimize his best efforts. This would have been particularly the case with the figure of Christ in *Christ's Charge to Peter*, or in other cases where he attempted to create relief or distance through *chiaroscuro* or *sfumato* effects, for the weavers were used to working with clear outlines and crisply defined forms and were not accustomed to creating effects of relief or recession through subtle gradations of light and shade. Thinking as a painter, and pitting himself in part against his rival, Raphael exercised his customary skills with little concession to those who would weave the tapestries.

Leaving aside the question of Raphael's influences, what are the specific elements of narrative design that Raphael brought to the tapestry cartoons, and what do these achieve? The first, and perhaps most obvious, is an almost exaggerated clarity of dramatic action. This is partly a result of the fact that the action is generally concentrated in the foreground, although that is not to say that there is no spatial depth or recession in the cartoons. However, the space is limited and well-defined, almost stage-like in nature, concentrated towards the front of the picture plane. Where there is dramatic recession into depth, as in *Christ's Charge to Peter* or *The Miraculous Draught of Fishes*, this takes place behind the figures in a way that does not remove attention from them. In other cartoons, such as *The Death of Ananias* or *The Conversion of the Proconsul*, deep space, as in landscape vistas, is glimpsed through windows, so as not to detract from the foreground action. Raphael conceived space, not as an object of artistic virtuosity, but as a neutral entity within which figures move or gesticulate, or across which they meet or interact. At the same time, the settings themselves are always carefully observed, either in relation to the biblical account, or in some way that underlines the narrative sequence. In *The Healing of the Lame Man*, for example, Raphael produces an imaginative reconstruction of the portico known as Solomon's, or the Beautiful Gate, at which the cripple was said to have sat, using Solomonic columns to create a series of aisles which allows him to separate the cripple and the apostles from the women bringing their children to the temple for purification.

In *Christ's Charge to Peter*, conflated from two texts, Raphael shows the action as taking place in front of water which must be simultaneously identified as the Lake of Gennesaret of the first text, and the Sea of Tiberias of the second. It must also be interpreted as a continuation of the lake shown in *The Miraculous Draught of Fishes*. In the former cartoon, the ups and downs of the architecture and trees in the landscape behind are carefully calculated to complement and further punctuate the rhythm of the apostles' heads. In *The Conversion of the Proconsul*, the central niche of the architecture encloses the Proconsul, while the columns around act as a foil for the columnar figures who stand and watch. In *The Death of Ananias* Raphael elaborated on the

Fig. 39. Michelangelo, detail of the Sistine Chapel ceiling, 1508–10, including *The Sacrifice of Noah* Fresco

biblical account to strengthen the meaning of the composition and clarify its action: the apostles are placed on a dais in front of a curtain and behind a kind of forum, not mentioned in the text, as a means of stressing their authority.

The clarity of action established in these ways is accentuated by two things – firstly, Raphael's eloquent use of gesture. While in many cases those gestures can carry resonances beyond the obvious, few are not self-explanatory in their most basic meaning, even to a modern audience. In other words, while the complexities of the narratives may not always be immediately apparent, the basic action is usually self-evident. The gestures which he employs are transparently, even theatrically expressive of action, intention or emotion. Raphael frequently adds to this by the use of one or more choric figures, whose task it is to accentuate for the spectator the significance of each scene. In *The Death of Ananias* the two recoiling figures in the foreground help make clear that we are witnessing

Above:
Fig.40. Masaccio
The Tribute Money, *c*.1427
Fresco, Brancacci Chapel,
S. Maria del Carmine,
Florence

Right:
Fig.41. Masaccio
*The Death of Ananias and
the Distribution of Goods*,
c.1427
Fresco, Brancacci Chapel,
S. Maria del Carmine,
Florence

Ananias' death throes. In *The Conversion of the Proconsul*, the chorus of figures on the right makes a variety of gestures of pointing, questioning, and expressing amazement, which call attention to the blinded sorcerer who moves towards the spectator. Hands helplessly outstretched, he wanders as written in the Bible 'seeking some to lead him by the hand'. Moreover, Raphael's figures usually hold their arms and hands well away from the rest of their bodies, making their gestures into clear space, or against an accentuating background. This is particularly evident in *The Death of Ananias*, where the memory of Masaccio's *Tribute Money* (fig.40) and *Death of Ananias* (fig.41) in the Brancacci Chapel, Florence, may have returned to Raphael's mind, in the repeated rhythm of the apostles' pointing hands. In many cases this technique results in clusters of juxtaposed and differently expressive hands which alert the spectator to the many different dimensions of each drama.[4]

The second feature which assists in the clarity of Raphael's narrative is the care with which he characterizes each figure – what we might call his observation of decorum, through both facial features and clothing. In *The Death of Ananias* the wealthy, horror-struck man in the foreground, with his fur-edged jacket, is clearly distinguished from the poorly dressed recipients of alms on the left. On the right, Ananias' wife, Sapphira, dressed in a radiant, multi-coloured gown, continues to count her coins, unaware of the dramatic central events. Not knowing of Ananias' fate, Sapphira also kept back part of her wealth, acquired from the sale of property, and three hours after him was similarly struck dead.

In *Christ's Charge to Peter*, each apostle is dressed in accordance with his station, the most ornate clothing being left to the youngest, for

4. Raphael was almost certainly influenced in his use of gesture, and in his compositions, by Alberti's treatise *On Painting*, of 1435.

In *The Conversion of the Proconsul*, the composition is particularly interesting in this respect. The dominant figure is the blinded sorcerer Elymas, while Paul stands to one side, a monumental figure who dwarfs the Proconsul, Sergius Paulus, as he points a warning hand towards him. The moment of conversion is not yet achieved – the Proconsul raises his hands in a gesture which simultaneously expresses amazement and disbelief – his right hand, juxtaposed with Paul's commanding gesture seems also a vain attempt to fend off the apostle's presence, while with downturned mouth he watches the stumbling figure before him. Although the conversion of the Proconsul is the actual conclusion of the story, from the viewer's aspect the dominant figures are Paul and Elymas and the crowd of astonished onlookers.

In *The Sacrifice at Lystra*, Raphael focuses on a moment of extreme tension, before Paul halts the impending sacrifice. The figure in the centre of the composition stands with his axe ready to fall, while others behind him still pay homage to the two saints on the podium with their hands clasped in adoration. Raphael concentrates rather on Paul's anger as he rents his garments in despair addressing, not the main crowd but the single figure below him (fig.42). In this moment of confusion, only one figure in the crowd seems to respond to Paul's wrath and the entreaties of Barnabas behind him, leaning forward in an attempt to halt the executioner. Yet the power of Paul's wrath and his impending chastisement of the Lystrians for their idolatry are implicit in his angry and powerful gesture and clouded countenance.

In *The Healing of the Lame Man* Raphael chooses the moment before the cripple is raised, the moment Peter, with John, grasps one of the cripple's hands and raises his own in blessing, saying 'Look on us. And he [the cripple] gave heed unto them, expecting to receive something from them'. Before the moment of cure, the onlookers crane forward to watch the outcome of the encounter.

In *Paul Preaching at Athens*, Raphael shows the saint surrounded by a crowd of largely sceptical Athenians, not yet swayed by the power of his speech, with the exception of the two figures placed strategically closest to the observer, and slightly larger than life, Dionysius the Areopagite and a woman named Damaris, who are recorded in the Bible as believers. It is also interesting to note that Paul does not look at the crowd he is addressing, but raises his eyes to heaven, as if to stress the divinely inspired nature of his eloquence.

In *The Miraculous Draught of Fishes*, which is slightly different in kind, Raphael again chooses a moment of some complexity, before Christ names Peter a fisher of men, and when Peter, having questioned Christ's command to let down his nets, kneels and says to the Lord,

Fig.43. Raphael
Study for *Christ's Charge to Peter* (counterproof)
Red chalk, 25.8 x 37.1cm
Royal Library, Windsor Castle

5. On the drawings for the cartoons see F. Ames-Lewis, *The Draftsman Rafael*, New Haven and London, 1986, pp.126–136 and P. Joannides, *The Drawings of Raphael*, Oxford, 1983, pp.23, 102 and 222–5.

'Depart from me, for I am a sinful man, O Lord'. At the same time, the apostle behind him, as if unaware of this intimate encounter, seeks his own dialogue with Christ, expressing amazement at the catch, while others struggle to haul the fish on board.

Arriving at these exceptional compositions can have been no easy task for Raphael, especially as he was designing them in reverse.[5] While some drawings survive for each cartoon, with the exception of *The Stoning of Stephen* the very patchiness of their survival makes it virtually impossible to trace Raphael's ideas for a composition in a coherent sequence from beginning to end. Similarly, the involvement of Raphael's assistants in the making of the surviving drawings makes it doubly difficult to be certain about their status – some may be copies or adjustments of lost originals by the master. It cannot be assumed, therefore, that they were the graphic solutions on which final compositions were based.

Examples of the types of drawings that survive are *garzone* or *bottega* studies, made using workshop assistants posing as models, which Raphael used to work out the initial arrangements of figures –

such as the *garzone* study for *Christ's Charge to Peter* illustrated here (fig.43). Like many of these *garzone* studies, this one was executed in red chalk, so that it could be counterproofed, in other words an impression made of it in reverse, so that Raphael could test the direction of the composition as in the tapestry. Other, similar studies for *Christ's Charge to Peter*, demonstrate that it took Raphael several attempts to arrive at the commanding stance and gesture of Christ as it appears in the cartoon. There also survives a number of highly finished *modelli* in different media, such as that illustrated here for *The Conversion of the Proconsul*, the authorship of which is uncertain (fig.44). Here the artist also seems concerned with the distribution of light and shade.

Surprisingly, what are lacking among the extant drawings are detailed studies for individual heads or figures, or for the fall of drapery. This may be because Raphael simply concentrated his energies on solving the problems of design, taking into account the reversal of the composition that would take place in the tapestries. Nonetheless, it is hard to believe that the exquisite heads in *Christ's Charge to Peter*, or those such as that of the cripple in *The Healing of the Lame Man* could have been executed without the aid of some fairly detailed studies, especially given the rudimentary nature of much of the underdrawing.

In addition to working out his thoughts through drawing, Raphael was able to draw on a wealth of other influences and experience, not

Fig.44. Raphael (?)
Modello for *The Conversion of the Proconsul*
Silverpoint, white heightening, brown wash, pen and brown ink, 27 x 35.5cm
Royal Library, Windsor Castle

least that of his own work in the Stanze. The influence of Michelangelo has already been mentioned, but Raphael also drew on the broader tradition of Florentine narrative painting and fresco cycles with which he was familiar. His use of space, the blocky simplicity of his forms and unfussy drapery irresistibly recall the example of Giotto, especially in *Paul Preaching at Athens*, while Masaccio's skill in economical story-telling and broad simple gestures is evident in *The Death of Ananias*. Leonardo's ability to orchestrate and coordinate groups of expressive figures, and his emphasis on the dramatic power of gesture, demonstrated in a work such as his unfinished *Adoration of the Magi*, must also have been influential.

There are also sources, quotations and reminiscences of a more recondite kind, which must have given particular pleasure to Leo. The foreground composition of *The Miraculous Draught of Fishes* has been shown to derive from an illumination in an eleventh-century Greek Gospel-Book in Leo's private library, while both *Christ's Charge to Peter* and *The Healing of the Lame Man* take aspects of their composition from a relief on the Ciborium of Sixtus IV. The idea of placing the apostles on a rostrum, backed by a curtain, in *The Death of Ananias*, was derived from a relief on the classical Arch of Constantine, showing one of the orations of the Emperor Augustus.[6] In August 1515 Leo had appointed Raphael to undertake an archaeological reconstruction of ancient Rome. The artist's knowledge of the antique was profound, and similar quotations from antique statues and buildings abound throughout the cartoons, both adding authenticity and affording immense pleasure to the tapestries' learned audience.

The narrative design of the cartoons is inextricably bound up with Raphael's use of colour which is also one of the most interesting features of their execution. It has already been suggested that Raphael coloured the cartoons more fully and in more detail than was strictly necessary for the weavers, and that, in the context of tapestry cartoons, this was quite unusual. The paint is relatively thick, opaque and well bound, and the colouring finished in places with some intricacy. What makes this particularly interesting is the fact that the colouring of the cartoons is dramatically different from that of the finished tapestries, and to compare the two comes as something of a shock. The cartoons and the tapestries (figs 14–20) appear to employ completely different colour ranges.

Talking about colour is difficult, for many colours are liable to fading and alteration and we cannot therefore be sure about their original appearance. The cartoons in fact seem relatively well-preserved in this respect, having been kept away from the light in boxes or behind curtains for much of their existence. Nevertheless, many of the colours

6. Shearman, op. cit., pp.118–124.

Fig.45. Detail of *Christ's Charge to Peter* (cartoon)

will inevitably have lost their intensity, especially some reds and pinks, and many areas have lost the highlights that would have given them added vivacity. Indeed there are areas where it is possible to see even without the benefit of technical investigation that some colours have faded. In *The Death of Ananias* the upper part of the robe of the apostle distributing alms on the left has become virtually transparent, while the lower part of his robe is a discoloured brown. The curtain behind the apostles, now a muddy brown with little visible definition, contains streaks of green that indicate it was once a different colour, or has since been retouched (fig.45). The best known example of change in the cartoons appears in *The Miraculous Draught of Fishes*, where the reflection of Christ's now whitish robe in the water appears pink, suggesting that his robe was originally painted in a red lake pigment which has subsequently faded, while the reflection itself was painted in the more stable vermilion. A similar effect of fading has occurred in the pinkish sack carried by the right-hand observer in *The Death of*

Fig.46.
Christ's Charge to Peter
Tapestry, reverse
Vatican Museums, Rome

7. Pigment samples from the cartoons are currently being analysed by Josephine Darrah. I am grateful for her advice in this respect.

Ananias. In *The Conversion of the Proconsul*, scientific analysis has revealed that the pale robe of the man on the extreme right was painted with a wide range of pigments, including indigo and orpiment, and was probably bright green. The underneath of Elymas' forward sleeve was a pale pink, while his leggings were a more intense mauve.[7] Other apparent anomalies, which may be explained by future pigment analysis, occur in *The Healing of the Lame Man*. In the woman with a baby to the right of centre, for example, her garment is starkly divided between a brown area on the left, probably intended to suggest or intensify shadow, and a pale blue on the right. It thus seems likely that a glaze or thin layer of another colour, now faded, originally covered and united the two areas. The garment of the cripple below her is now made up of patches of indeterminate colour, yet a single patch of bright blue above his belt, probably a later retouch in blue verditer, suggests that his clothing was also a definite blue at some point, and that this has subsequently faded.

Fig.47. Detail of fig.46

In comparison the tapestries have suffered extensive fading and discolouration. A view of the back of the tapestry of *Christ's Charge to Peter* during restoration, where the colours have been protected from the light by lining, gives some idea of their original vividness and brilliancy, and of how much the balance of colours has been changed through the passage of time (fig.46). Most conspicuous perhaps is the relative loss of the yellows, a fugitive dye, and consequently of the greens, which would have given the originals much of their richness (fig.14). In the areas of landscape, the green of the cartoons often appears as a kind of undistinguished ochre, or as a bluish tone with highlights of gold; true greens are relatively rare. A detail of the back of *Christ's Charge to Peter* gives some idea of the green tonalities that must once have been present (fig.47). There is also a loss of variation in tone of some of the larger areas of blue.

Even taking these factors into account, it is clear that the weavers took a different approach to colour from that employed by Raphael. The tapestries are bright with vivid, primary colours, and extensive use of scarlets and blues, far removed from the soft, harmonious more pastel tones employed in the cartoons. Nor does their use of silver-gilt thread bear any relation to indications, such as white highlights, visible on the cartoons, while the subtle shot-colour effects employed by Raphael, now sometimes hard to detect, were most often ignored. In *Paul Preaching at Athens*, the rich variety of subtle tones and *cangiante* (shot, or changing) colours used for the onlookers in the cartoon are all but lost in the tapestry (fig.15), while the tapestries of *The Sacrifice at Lystra* (fig.16) and *The Healing of the Lame Man* (fig.17) are largely dominated by simple reds and blues. Nor is there anything in the tapestries that matches the soft variety of harmonious colour in *Christ's Charge to Peter*, where Raphael unites the composition not just by gesture, but by the crescendo of colour from the cool white of Christ's robe, through the mid-green robes in the centre to the warm red garment of the apostle at the end of the line. In the tapestry, the composition becomes more a staccato rhythm of brilliant reds and blues.

An illuminating reflection on colour which has some relevance here appears in Vasari's technical prefaces. Discussing the way in which colour should be used, he wrote:

...let the colours of the lights of the drapery be delicate

and similar to the tints of the flesh, either yellowish or reddish, violet or purple, making the depths either green or blue or purple or yellow, provided that they tend to a harmonious sequence in the rounding of the figures with their shadows...in the same manner the colours should be employed with so much harmony that a dark and a light are not left unpleasantly contrasted in light and shade, save only in the case of projections, which are those shadows that the figures throw on one another...and these again when they occur must be painted with sweetness and harmony, because he who throws them into disorder makes that picture look like a coloured carpet...rather than blended flesh or soft clothing or other things that are light, delicate and sweet.[8]

Similarly, Giovan Battista Armenini, in his *True Precepts of Painting* commented, 'A harmonious composition is neither so gaudy that it looks like a coloured tapestry, nor is it so sombre that the true tints of flesh or nearby objects cannot be discerned.'[9] It is interesting that both writers use the analogy with carpets and tapestries to illustrate their idea of an unmodulated colour composition, such as Raphael attempted to avoid.

The weavers' alterations are important, not least because Raphael used colour for both iconographic means and compositional balance and, with the alteration of colour, these are often disrupted – even though the weavers did attempt in some cases to create an equivalent balance in terms of light and dark. Colour is used by Raphael to identify and characterize key figures, especially Peter and Paul. In the cartoons, Peter is invariably dressed in a yellow mantle over a blue robe, while Paul wears red over green. It is thus surprising that, in three cases, the weavers dressed Peter also in red, in the face of iconographic conventions.

In a few cases, such as that of *Christ's Charge to Peter*, there may have been a logic to these changes. The weavers may have felt a yellow mantle would not have been sufficiently distinguishable from the ground colour against which Peter kneels, and there are other cases where the alteration of a colour may have been necessitated by the importance of keeping figures distinct from each other or their surroundings. Unable to use subtle variations of light and shade, as used by Raphael, the weavers may at times have had to substitute differences of colour at odds with the cartoons themselves.

In *The Conversion of the Proconsul* Raphael's careful orchestration of colours is again altered in the tapestry (fig.18). In the cartoon, only Paul wears red, balanced by a few touches of red on the other side,

8. *Vasari on Technique*, op. cit., p.219.
9. Armenini, op. cit., p.176.

Left:
Fig.48. Detail of fig.46

Right:
Fig.49. Detail of fig.14

such as the boots or hats of the onlookers. The Proconsul wears a golden but subdued robe that blends in with the architecture behind. This single splash of red emphasizes Paul's majesty and stresses his presence. In the tapestry, however, the Proconsul is also given a vivid red mantle, disrupting a subtle compositional and iconographic point. Other points of red are increased, while Paul's green undergarment becomes a vivid blue.

To suggest that the alterations to the colours were purely the result of artists working in different media would be to over-simplify the point. It is tempting to conclude that the weavers were simply not able to match Raphael's subtle colour effects, painted in distemper, with their existing range of dyes. Yet while this may be partially true, it is certainly not wholly the case. A detail of the back of *Christ's Charge to Peter* shows that they originally rendered the white robe worn by Christ in the cartoon in a delicate mauve, embroidered with stars, as subtle as anything achieved by Raphael (fig.48). In some cases they also produced stunning shot-colour effects of their own, as in the blue and yellow robe of the woman with the baby in *The Healing of the Lame Man.*

The weavers' desire to exercise their own freedom is also evident in other, smaller ways, as they made the heads and hair colour of the apostles in *Christ's Charge to Peter* much more uniform (fig.49). They also added considerably to the decoration of the cartoons, for example in the embroidered stars on Christ's robe in *Christ's Charge to Peter*, on the borders to the clothing of Paul and the Proconsul in *The Conversion of the Proconsul*, and in details of the foliage in *Christ's Charge to Peter*.

Fig. 50. Michelangelo
The Ancestors of Christ,
1508–10
Fresco
Sistine Chapel, Rome

It is thus more likely that the weavers simply had their own ideas about the choice and distribution of colour, and of gilt thread, based both on their own decorative tradition and also perhaps on a sense of how the tapestries would look when lit by candles or oil-lamps. Indeed, they almost certainly thought of this aspect of the weaving as their own province, rather than that of the painter, and one of the ways in which they expected to demonstrate their skill and artistic freedom. Their attraction to red may also have been influenced by economic considerations as kermes, the red dye used was the most expensive in their repertoire. Like ultramarine in painting, it could therefore have connotations of richness and majesty, and the red robes of Peter and the Proconsul could have been adopted to lend the figures additional status, while stressing the overall magnificence of the tapestries.

In terms of Raphael's approach to the colouring of the cartoons, the analyses that have been carried out to date suggest that there was nothing unusual about his choice of pigments and that he did not adopt a radically different approach to the cartoons from that in his other contemporary works. This in itself is significant, however, for he would surely have been familiar with the approach to colour conventionally

Fig.51. Michelangelo
The Ancestors of Christ,
1508–10
Fresco
Sistine Chapel, Rome

used in tapestry. He clearly chose to make no concessions and painted the cartoons as a painter, rather than as a designer.

One reason for Raphael's approach to colour must surely have been his sense of competition with Michelangelo's Sistine Ceiling, the colours of which have been properly revealed by the recent restoration. Especially in the figures of the prophets and sibyls, and the ancestors of Christ, Michelangelo used an astonishing range of virtuoso colour effects, particularly *cangiante* colours, also applying the colour in broad, simple washes as, for the most part, does Raphael (figs 50 and 51). While it is true that to an extent the same effects were apparent in the fifteenth-century frescoes, notably the figures of the Popes, it is in the lunettes of the ceiling that they stand out most clearly, and there can be little doubt that Raphael wanted the tapestries to hold their own against Michelangelo as a colourist. The ravishing, if damaged garment of Sapphira in *The Death of Ananias* which changes from green to yellow, to purple and blue (fig.52); the delicate yellow highlights on the purple robe of the aged Athenian in *Paul Preaching at Athens*; the multi-coloured garments of the Lystrians in *The Sacrifice at Lystra* and the shot-colour gown of the woman with the basket in *The Healing of the*

Fig. 52. Detail of *The Death of Ananias* (cartoon)

Lame Man are just some of many examples that testify to Raphael's concern in this respect, and he must surely have hoped that the weavers would follow his lead, just as he may have hoped that the cartoons themselves would survive to enhance his reputation. Yet in reality, when lit by candlelight, rather than calling out to the colours of the ceiling, the bright colours and silver-gilt thread of the tapestries must have shone like so many precious jewels across the surface of the wall, amply fulfilling Leo's quest for magnificence.

There remain a number of unanswered questions about the cartoons. Some periods in their history are still not fully understood, and there are technical questions, such as the exact manner in which they were assembled, which may never be completely resolved. What is clear from our investigations is that Raphael looked on the cartoons as more than designs for tapestry. The care with which the paper surfaces are put together; the rarity of tears or repairs originating in Raphael's workshop; the lack of major *pentimenti* or alterations made either in under-

93

drawing or by the application of patches; the care with which the pigments are combined; the balance of colours and tones; the attention to detail in landscapes, garments and architectural settings: these are just some of the features that indicate the work that Raphael invested in these potentially short-lived objects. In many respects, he approached them in the same way as his other commissions of the period, particularly his works in fresco, and there seems often to be little distinction between them in terms of colour, handling of paint and the use of composition and gesture.

It may be that Raphael simply chose not to distinguish between the cartoons and his other works and continued working in his customary way. But this in itself is significant for it shows that, at a time when he and his workshop were busy with numerous other commissions, he chose not to save time by economizing on the care with which he carried out the cartoons, even though he would have known that they could either disappear, or become damaged and destroyed.

It is also clear that Raphael made few, if any, concessions to the needs of the tapestry-weavers or to the conventional style of tapestry design as he would have known it from other examples. This was still in many ways anti-pictorial and anti-illusionistic with an emphasis on rich materials, bright colours and decorative surface pattern. In the cartoons, however, Raphael adhered to the qualities valued in contemporary painting – spatial clarity, dramatic gesture, harmonious composition, modulated colour and an emphasis on the illusion of three dimensions, especially in the painting of the figure. In these respects, the cartoons are the natural successors, not only to Raphael's own fresco cycles in the Stanze, but to the great tradition of Florentine fresco cycles from Giotto, through Masaccio and Ghirlandaio. The same tradition informed much of Michelangelo's painting on the Sistine Ceiling, a fact of which Raphael was very much aware.

Whatever Raphael imagined would be the fate of his cartoons, their style and quality make clear his awareness of the importance of the tapestry commission. This was not only a recognition of the patron and the setting but also of the fact that the design of the tapestries would have to stand comparison with Michelangelo's ceiling. By imposing on the weavers the values of early sixteenth-century painting, Raphael tried to ensure that his own skills and talents remained clearly in evidence and that he was seen to equal Michelangelo in colour, composition and the painting of the figure. By lavishing on the cartoons the full range of his expertise and inventiveness, he also produced a set of independent works whose intrinsic beauty and fascination have ensured their extraordinary survival.

SELECT BIBLIOGRAPHY

Ames-Lewis, Francis, *The Draftsman Rafael*, New Haven and London, 1986

Armenini, Giovanni Battista, *On the True Precepts of Painting* (1586), ed. E. Olszewski, Burt Franklin and Co., 1977

Bambach, Carmen, 'Michelangelo's Cartoon for the *Crucifixion of St Peter* Reconsidered', *Master Drawings*, vol.XXV, no.2, March 1988, pp.131–41

Campbell, Tom, 'School of Raphael tapestries in the collection of Henry VIII', *Burlington Magazine*, vol.CXXXVIII, no.115, February 1996, pp.69–79

Cavallo, Adolfo Salvatore, *Medieval Tapestries in the Metropolitan Museum, New York*, New York, 1993

Coffinet, Julien, *Arachne ou l'art de la tapisserie*, Geneva, 1971

Davidson, Bernice, 'The *Furti di Giove* Tapestries designed by Perino del Vaga for Andrea Doria', *Art Bulletin*, September 1988, vol.LXX, no.3, pp.424–49

Delmarcel, Guy et al., *Autour des Fructus Belli: une tapisserie de Bruxelles du XVI siècle*, Paris, 1992

Ettlinger, Lee, *The Sistine Chapel before Michelangelo*, Oxford, 1965

Ferrero Viale, Mercedes, *Arazzi Italiani del Cinquecento*, 2nd ed., Milan, 1982

Gilbert, Creighton E., 'Are the ten tapestries a complete series or a fragment?', *Studi su Raffaello; atti del congresso internazionale di studi*, Urbino-Florence, 1984, pp.533–50

Gombrich, Ernst et al., *Giulio Romano*, Milan, 1989

Golzio, Vincenzo, *Raffaello nei documenti, nelle testimonianze dei contemporanei e nella letteratura del suo secolo*, Vatican City, 1936

Hirst, Michael, 'I disegni di Michelangelo per la *Battaglia di Cascina*', *Tecnica e Stile: esempi di pittura murale del Rinascimento italiano*, ed. E. Borsook and F. Superbi Gioffredi, Milan, 1986, vol.I, pp.43–58

Joannides, Paul, *The Drawings of Raphael with a complete catalogue*, Oxford, 1983

Jobé, Joseph ed., *The Art of Tapestry*, London, 1965

Jones, Roger and Penny, Nicholas, *Raphael*, New Haven and London, 1983

Oberhuber, Konrad, *Il cartone per la Scuola di Atene*, Milan, 1972

Pietrangeli, Carlo et al., *The Sistine Chapel. The Art, the History and the Restoration*, New York, 1986

Plesters, Joyce, 'Raphael's Cartoons for the Vatican Tapestries: A Brief Report on the Materials, Technique and Condition', in *The Princeton Raphael Symposium. Science in the Service of Art History*, ed. John Shearman and Marcia Hall, Princeton, 1990, pp.111–24

Shearman, John, *Only Connect...Art and the Spectator in the Italian Renaissance*, Princeton, 1992

Shearman, John, *Raphael's Cartoons in the collection of Her Majesty the Queen and the tapestries for the Sistine Chapel*, London, 1972

Thomson, William George, *A History of Tapestry from the Earliest Times until the Present Day*, 2nd ed., London, 1930

Vasari, Giorgio, *Le Vite de' Più Eccellenti Pittori, Scultori ed Architettori*, ed. G. Milanesi, 9 vols, Florence, 1878

Vasari on Technique, trans. L. Maclehose, ed. G. Baldwin Brown, New York, 1960

Wolk-Simon, Linda, 'Fame, *Paragone* and the Cartoon', *Master Drawings*, vol.30, no.1, 1992, pp.61–82

Index

*Numbers in **bold** type refer to illustrations*